PSYCHOANALYTIC INQUIRY

A Topical Journal for Mental Health Professionals

Volume 13 1993 Number 4

Locating Transference: Actuality and Illusion in the Psychoanalytic Encounter

JOSEPH D. LICHTENBERG
Dedication........257
GAIL S. REED, Ph.D. and HOWARD B. LEVINE, M.D., *Issue Editors*
Prologue........259
ELSA FIRST, M.A.
Countertransference Strain and the Use of the Analyst........264
MICHAEL FELDMAN, F.R.C. Psych.
Aspects of Reality, and the Focus of Interpretation........274
ALAN Z. SKOLNIKOFF, M.D.
The Analyst's Experience in the Psychoanalytic Situation: A Continuum Between Objective and Subjective Reality........296
STANLEY L. OLINICK, M.D.
Structural Actualities of the Transference and Their Effects on the Analyst's Functions........310
FREDERIC J. LEVINE, Ph.D.
Unconscious Fantasy and Theories of Technique........326
AXEL HOFFER, M.D.
Is Love in the Analytic Relationship "Real"?........343
ANDRÉ HAYNAL, M.D. and ERNST FALZEDER, Ph.D.
Slaying the Dragons of the Past or Cooking the Hare in the Present: A Historical View on Affects in the Psychoanalytic Encounter........357
MARTIN S. BERGMANN
Reality and Psychic Reality in Ernst Kris's Last Papers: An Attempt to Update His Findings........372
HOWARD B. LEVINE, M.D., *Issue Editor*
Actuality and Illusion in the Transference: A Brief Discussion........384
GAIL S. REED, Ph.D., *Issue Editor*
Epilogue: Actuality, Illusion, and Clinical Authority........391

Routledge
Taylor & Francis Group
New York London

Routledge is an imprint of the
Taylor & Francis Group, an informa business

PSYCHOANALYTIC INQUIRY

ISSN 0735-1690

Dedication

At the suggestion of the Issue Editors and with the enthusiastic agreement of the *Psychoanalytic Inquiry* editorial board, this issue is dedicated to Nathaniel London, M.D., 1927–1989.

Nat London and I grew up a few blocks apart in a neighborhood of reasonably affluent second- or third-generation Jews from Germany and Eastern Europe. In that setting intense discussions of capitalism, socialism, and communism, of the New Deal, the depression, and the threat of fascism, of orthodoxy and reformed Judiasm and atheism were commonplace. In other words, we grew up in a world of lively dialectic, to put a toney reference to it or Talmudic quibbling once removed, to give it its origin.

It was no surprise, then, that Nat the doctor, the analyst, and the institute director became a major challenger of stated doctrines. Nor were we surprised to hear him ask questions like, Is any prevailing view of schizophrenia acceptable in itself? Is the concept of the transference neurosis evolving or obsolete? Nor to hear him answering—against a prevailing trend—It is evolving. Nor to find him becoming interested in self psychology but soon asking, If empathy predominates, then where is the place for the worthy adversary?—and then telling a tale of the therapeutic effect on the transference of an episode of arm wrestling. Nor his challenging admonition that self in self psychology is as apt to become anthropomorphic as was ego in ego psychology.

Finally, I recall the heated phone calls we had about his insistence on using the word ludic in the title of his wonderful paper, "On Play Elements in Regression," which began the first issue of *Psychoanalytic Inquiry*. Ludic, he said, emphasized a special, nonserious quality of the interactional context of a transference neurosis. Play, I said, played better to the readers we hoped to appeal to. And so it went, the nonserious joy of dialectic about the serious issues of our day in psychoanalysis: What are the play/ludic aspects of the transference and what are those that are not (serious/actual)? We can all give thanks for the time we had Nat's imaginative creativity with us. The world continues to need people like Nat, who challenge so productively.

Joseph D. Lichtenberg, M.D.
Editor-in-Chief

Prologue: Actuality and Illusion in the Psychoanalytic Encounter

THE INTERRELATION BETWEEN ACTUALITY AND ILLUSION within the clinical encounter is a subject that has influenced the theory and practice of psychoanalysis since its beginnings, particularly with regard to how clinicians identify and construe the transference.

After he revised his theory in terms of psychic reality and the Oedipus complex, Freud continued to focus theoretical attention away from the pathogenic actuality or *event* to the illusion, or unconscious fantasy linked to phase-specific unconscious wishes. There is ample evidence of his ongoing clinical concern with the objective event as well as with the subjective meaning to which it gave rise (Freud, 1918; Kardiner, 1977; Levine, 1990). Despite that evidence, after Freud's death the idea that meaning developed from the *reciprocal relation between inner and outer event* was in practice often ignored in favor of a simplified version of fantasy so that there was more than a kernel of truth in the charge that classical psychoanalysis—as opposed to some classical analysts—did not pay sufficient attention to actual traumatic childhood events and their impact on the individual.

In retrospect, it is curious that a dichotomous relationship between actuality and illusion became so entrenched. There has always been a current in psychoanalytic thinking in which actual events are not only interpreted in terms of an individual's fantasy systems but are simultaneously seen to organize and influence those unconscious fantasy systems that we here refer to under the more general term of illusion (Reed, 1993). Yet, at times it seemed that the emphasis on illusion had become so one-sided that illusion was used to define psychoanalysis (in Hartmann's [1959, p. 35] definition of psychoanalysis as the systematic study of self-deception) and to differentiate patients who are analyzable from those who are not analyzable (in the concept of those patients able to sustain the "as-if" quality of the transference). At the extreme of favoring illusion over actuality, moreover, good technique has been equated with abstinence and the analyst with a mirror. In traditional formulations of the analytic situation, it was rarely considered that an interpretation, however correct the technique in which it was embodied, might constitute an action and an actuality for the patient, or that the analyst himself continually has transferences to his patient.

Traditionally, theorists have tended to distinguish actuality and illusion within the psychoanalytic situation by creating a dichotomy between action and existence, on the one hand, and the attribution of meaning, on the other. Thus "actuality" came to refer roughly to the data of external perception, to any action on the part of analyst or patient and, by extension, to aspects of the external world that are part of the analytic encounter, and "illusion" came to reflect the operation of the individual's fantasy function. That is, it involves the attribution of meaning to a particular actuality as that actuality has been represented in the psyche. It can involve the interpretations of both analyst and analysand (Arlow, 1969).

Yet in recent years we have become increasingly aware that the separation of actuality and illusion is not as clear-cut and straightforward as had been assumed. A sharp distinction between internal and external, objective and subjective, is a residue of nineteenth-century positivism, belied both by Freud's discovery of the unconscious—an actuality though not an external, objective, observable entity—and by clinical practice. Many analysts accordingly no longer subscribe to ideas that allow for such a precise separation between observer and observed. We are now acutely aware that the analyst as well as the patient is subjectively influenced in his or her observations. This awareness is reflected in our greater sensitivity to the ubiquity and implications of countertransference phenomena (Abend, 1989) and in the expectation that the analyst's transferences will influence his work with a patient (McLaughlin, 1981).

With the comfort gone that was once derived from the belief that illusion was the property and problem of the patient alone, we are all more apt to see perception and memory as continually subject to unconsciously motivated interpretations and revisions. Given this intermixing of actuality and illusion in both parties to the analytic dyad, we asked our contributors to describe where in this clinical complexity they located actuality and illusion in the treatments they conduct.

How one identifies the patient's actual data, how one interprets them and the relation of both to the analyst's stance toward his own experience of the analytic encounter is one crucial area along this axis of actuality/illusion. Another is the continuing debate about the relation between transference and the therapeutic or working alliance (Zetzel, 1956; Greenson, 1965; Brenner, 1980; Panel, 1992). We encouraged our contributors to address the question of whether such a distinction is sound or is a result of the analyst's illusory apprehension of the patient's wishes to actualize the transference.

Another area we asked them to address concerned the analyst's method of sorting out and understanding the origins of countertransference feelings and the actions, interpretative or otherwise, to which these give rise. For some analysts, particularly those who believe in and use the concept of projective identification (Klein, 1946), the action of the analyst may more usefully be conceptualized as belonging to the illusion of the patient.

To the extent that it is inherent in our definition of the transference that the patient will misperceive us and the analysis, we should expect sometimes to arrive at a strong difference of opinion between analyst and analysand as to what is going on. When this difference becomes painfully intractable, we may even say that the patient has a psychotic transference. In such situations, we are apt to think that we are "right" about whatever is at issue and the patient is "wrong," misperceiving the present (us) in terms of the past, as an aspect of his or her self-deception. But how we are to know that we have not been clinging to an idiosyncratic interpretation of events, perhaps for our own unconscious reasons? Given a patient whose capacity to separate fantasy from reality is significantly, although perhaps temporarily, impaired, these situations become overwhelmingly difficult to negotiate. The widening scope of analysis has probably played a double role in our new, if unsettled, perspective. It has contributed to our readiness to ask these difficult questions and has made more acute the need to attempt to answer them. We invited our contributions to describe their approach to this difficult clinical problem.

We think our contributors have responded to our challenge with enterprise, skill, creativity, and grit. At the clinical level, Elsa First recounts a treatment evolution from a "mutual embroilment" to a phase in which transference interpretation became possible; Michael Feldman describes the ingredients in his decision of when to intervene and what to remark upon; and Alan Skolnikoff describes the unrecognized intersubjectivity of the middle phase of analysis. In the arena of clinical theory, Stanley Olinick argues for a category of subjective response in the analyst that is based on the analyst's actual response to structural properties inherent in the patient's transference; Frederic Levine describes certain superego conflicts in analysts and shows their relation to theories of technique; and Axel Hoffer distinguishes between the actuality of the patient's transference love and the use to which analysis puts it. From a historical perspective, André Haynal and Ernst Falzeder discuss Freud's and Ferenczi's characteristically different reactions to the painful recognition of the actualities of the analyst's transference feelings toward patients, which in the early days of psychoanalysis led to some serious and well-known transgressions; and Martin Bergmann explicates the seminal contribution of Ernst Kris to the conceptualization of memory and elaborates its implications for technique. The editors, individually, have the last words.

REFERENCES

Abend, S. (1989). Countertransference and psychoanalytic technique. *Psychoanal. Quart.*, 58:374–395.

Arlow, J. A. (1969). Fantasy, memory, and reality testing. *Psychoanal. Quart.*, 38:28–51.

Brenner, C. (1980). Working and therapeutic alliance. In: *Psychoanalytic Explorations of Technique*, ed. H. Blum. New York: Int. Univ. Press, pp. 137–159.

Freud, S. (1918). From the history of an infantile neurosis. *S.E.*, 17.
Greenson, R. (1965). The working alliance and the transference neurosis. *Psychoanal. Quart.*, 34:155–181.
Hartmann, H. (1959). Psychoanalysis as a scientific theory. In: *Essays in Ego Psychology*. New York: Int. Univ. Press, 1964, pp. 318–349.
Kardiner, A. (1977). *My Analysis with Freud*. New York: Norton.
Klein, M. (1946). Notes on some schizoid mechanisms. In: *Developments in Psychoanalysis*, ed. M. Klein, P. Heiman, S. Isaacs and J. Riviere. London: Hogarth Press, 1952, pp. 292–320.
Levine, H. B. (1990). Introduction. In: *Adult Analysis and Childhood Sexual Abuse*, ed. H. B. Levine. Hillsdale, NJ: The Analytic Press, pp. 3–20.
McLaughlin, J. (1981). Transference, psychic reality and countertransference. *Psychoanal. Quart.*, 50:639–664.
Panel (1992). Freudian and Kleinian theory: A dialogue of comparative perspectives. H. B. Levine, reporter, *J. Amer. Psychoanal. Assn.*, 40:801–826.
Reed, G. S. (1992). On the value of explicit reconstruction. *Psychoanal. Quart.*, 62:52–73.
Zetzel, E. R. (1956). Current concepts of transference. *Internat. J. Psycho-Anal.*, 37:369–376.

Gail S. Reed, Ph.D.
Howard B. Levine, M.D.
Issue Editors

Countertransference Strain and the Use of the Analyst

ELSA FIRST, M.A.

FOR MANY OF US, OUR WAY of analytic listening has shifted over the last 15 years or so. We listen to the patient, but along with this we listen to the dialogue in the consulting room, to discern what kind of relationship is perhaps being enacted between the two participants. We hope to use this information to help us recognize patterns of transference and countertransference or "role responsiveness" (Sandler, 1976). But in all this, what are we to call real, actual, or illusory? Having come this far from a positivist opposition of transference versus reality, how are we to orient ourselves? As a contribution to making the ambiguities of this question discussable in clinical terms, I here present material from an analytic patient for whom, for a while, only the analyst's perceived failings were real.

I want to highlight a moment when the patient could begin to experience transference as partly his own subjective contribution rather than primarily trying to prove that the analyst is "really" recreating a failure of the object. Prior to this, the patient had been trying to establish how much the analyst contained unwanted aspects of the patient, or of the patient's defensive, masochistic, identifications with the failing object. I see this moment as an example of a turning point which occurs in some analyses, particularly with some traumatized patients who do not start treatment able to do ordinary analytic work. In this example, the

Elsa First is a Training and Supervising Analyst, New York Freudian Society; she is on the faculty of the New York University Postdoctoral Program in Psychotherapy and Psychoanalysis.

analyst's capacity to contain the externalizations or projections seems to facilitate the emergence of a usable interpretable transference, i.e., one which the patient could begin to experience as transference. In Winnicott's language (1968), this might be a moment at which the patient became able (or more able) to make "use" of the analyst.[1]

In this brief presentation, I would like to trace a series of four samplings of interactions over a six-month period in a middle-phase of an analysis. I am attempting to give a two-person account of events around this turning point. The task of containing the patient's attributions or projections (or perceptions) in this instance included the analyst's implicitly taking responsibility for any characterological predisposition for the countertransference.

A brief statement of some clinical affinities in regard to analytic stance may be appropriate here, because how one defines neutrality, and what one recognizes as its correlate in the analyst's subjective state bears on how one defines countertransference and transference. Presumably we all try for a state that permits free-floating or evenly hovering attention. And presumably we also try for some balance or fluidity between engagement and disengagement. But characterological emphases in stance will differ, as do our ways of fine-tuning immediacy and distance, communality and separateness.

I believe the analyst's task is to maintain or recover or arrive at neutrality, but in a relaxed enough manner that we can be temporarily pulled off center. My idea of neutrality is retaining the capacity to stay, internally, in good contact with the patient. My sense of "staying in contact," seems close enough to the use of this idea in, for example, the writings of Rosenfeld (1987), who uses it as a baseline measure: a given analyst is more or less able to stay in contact with a given patient at any particular time. It seems to be a notion of accuracy of contact, which, I think is common in the discourse of the British Independents and some modern Kleinians, and serves, though perhaps not explicitly, as an operative definition of neutrality. It is *not* to be equated with sympathy or identification or empathy per se.

[1]In Kleinian terms it might be located as a move from a "paranoid" into a "depressive" position, in which internal experience is possible, and a capacity for guilt replaces blaming.

The first sampling is an example of a countertransference enactment.[2] The enactment was this: the patient (male) was about to leave for a barely announced short vacation. At the end of the session, when she would not ordinarily initiate conversation, the analyst asked, "So where are you going this time?" He explained politely, at length, taking pains not to make the analyst seem unsophisticated, but he ended up somehow looking foolish and humiliated. A similar situation had been discussed in that very session: The patient had had an exchange with a female co-worker, and ended up feeling humiliated. The clarification had been offered: "It sounds like a situation in which you don't feel sure whether you are being appreciated and encouraged or mocked and humiliated." The patient felt this description fit.

The analyst noted that a very similar transaction had just been enacted between her and the patient. The rawness of this involuntary enactment contrasted with the careful attentiveness of the session, causing the analyst to appreciate the power of the evoked relationship and to sample the affects more thoroughly. Somehow, the analyst supposed, she had played the part of the competitive but handicapped colleague, or the competitive, envious, covertly sarcastic sibling. She then hypothesized that something was perhaps being enacted involving early sexual play with the sibling in which the patient started by feeling his own arousal was admired but ended humiliated. This was only a speculative and of course uninterpreted hunch. The evidence of countertransference startled the analyst and caused her to examine how she might have been provoked while being unable to notice it. She realized she also had been deflected from noticing the provocations by the patient's presenting himself as victimized. The analyst became more alert to provocations, and to the degree of her unconscious involvement. Several weeks later, the patient referred back to this exchange as "something strange," giving himself permission to think and speak about it.

There followed a period of several months marked by severe reproaches to the analyst for her indifference. The patient monitored breaches in the analytic frame or setting that meant to him a lack of the analyst's attentive concern and desire to see him.

[2]It was selected at random as the first example that came to my attention in a given week.

Examples were doors ajar to other rooms in the suite, the analyst arriving in the waiting room from outside or from another room in the suite rather than being calmly settled in her office whenever he arrived, a lightbulb out in an anteroom, a window open to street noise in the consulting room, a drawer being shut as he entered. Instead of being prepared and eager to receive him, and being concerned to protect him from intrusions, she was, he felt, telegraphing disarray and the primacy of other preoccupations, and making him feel that far from being able to express his anger with her, he should be taking care of her. The reproaches would crescendo in relentlessness, but their meaning for him could not be explored. He seemed to be trying to impress an acute experience of disregard on the analyst which he felt she could not appreciate.

At times he insisted that such lapses proved the analyst carried no memory of him and his needs. "You could not be remembering anything I said, or this would not be happening again."[3]

As he began to make considerable progress in his career and to test out the possibility of showing excitement or initiative in sessions, he took lapses in the management of the setting as proof that the analyst resented his progress, and wanted to undermine him. "I am just a yawn to you if you show up with a coffee cup after a good session."

At the height of this struggle, the patient had a dream. (This is our second sample.) The dream could be said to represent his fear of driving the analyst crazy or his fear that the analyst could not tolerate his recriminations and demands. (This dream followed a session the patient had missed through some acknowledged confusion on his part.) The dream takes place in the analyst's waiting room. The patient arrives for a session, but the analyst doesn't show up until the session is over. The waiting room fills with people whom the dreamer takes to be members of the analyst's family of origin; they look very worried that she is not there. When the analyst arrives these family members look at her "as if she is crazy, act as if they don't want to know her," and attack her with recriminations. "In the style of my family," the patient later explains, "let's tear the victim to shreds." In the dream, the analyst

[3]Months later, he was able to say, "If you do think of me when I am not here, that would mean you might rape me when I am here."

arrives looking confused and upset, and the patient says to her, "If you can't take responsibility for being here, perhaps we should part." The analyst in the dream then "goes to pieces, cries, and says, 'Maybe you are right, I can't handle this.' "

After relating the dream, the patient continued to be angry at the analyst for her behavior *in* the dream. "That's how I felt about you in the dream and that's how I'm feeling now. Why won't you do what you have to do to make me feel welcome!" He seemed to regard the dream as an oracular proof that the analyst's internal difficulties (as represented by her abusive family of origin in the dream) were interfering with his treatment. He also, on his own, understood it as conveying his fear that if he continued to reveal his complaints she would become more and more incapacitated. He related it to his childhood experiences of mother's collapses, which father provoked by attacking mother as inadequate, ugly, and crazy. It also led the patient to a franker communication of his underlying anxiety that the analyst would prove crazy, and he became able to observe his ongoing conflict over wishes to express criticism and dissent in the analysis.

Reporting that B, whom he was dating, complained of his exigence, he showed the beginnings of curiosity about himself: In the dream there had been an exigent and critical young man in the waiting room, wearing the patient's glasses. He had been convinced this must be the analyst's brother, but now he wondered whether it might be an aspect of himself.

The analyst meanwhile was prompted by the dream to consider whether the patient, perhaps by stimulating masochistic guilt in her, had caused her to collude in communicating unreadiness or cavalier aloofness, and resolved to watch this. As the setting for a while was maintained more faultlessly, in accord with the patient's wishes, the patient's ire fastened upon more minute details. During this general period, the patient also spontaneously recognized for the first time his wish to make his mother suffer painful guilt in retaliation for her disregard.

What I have described could be termed a sample of a period of "mutual embroilment" (Renik, in press). The patient seeks to externalize and enact rather than remember, by reproaching the analyst in a confusing and demoralizing way. The analyst cannot get a clear idea about what is happening in the interaction and is unable to feel satisfied with the analysis or her introspection. Is the patient provoking her so that she has more management lapses? Perhaps the patient has an accurate complaint about her unconscious counterresistance? Should she feel more or less guilty? The analyst saw as her task to hold the situation sufficiently in this state of uncertainty and muddling through, which meant to continue to be alert to opportunities to clarify it.

I turn now to the third sampling, a single session in which I think we can watch the analyst's containment of the sadomasochistic provocation.

The session began with a striking statement. "Things are going better everywhere else in my life. Sex is still a problem in my relationship with B, but we have started to talk. I feel it's coming down more and more to *our* relationship and some fundamental questions: Do you want me here or do you want to kill me?"

He tells a dream he had, following a missed session the day before. (He knew it was his own muddle that had caused him to miss the session, which had been rescheduled at his request. It was an emerging pattern that, when the analyst was without undue difficulty able to grant some request for rescheduling, he would sabotage it. He then had phoned at the session time, hastily interrupted that call, and when he had called back to explain, found the analyst's answering machine off. "I felt like you wanted to kill me," he says.

In the dream, he is given a disappointing gift, which is useless to him. The woman who gave the disappointing gift reappears with a gun and wants to kill him. "The whole thing is set up like an assassination. My gut feeling is, *that woman was you.*"

Here he insists the analyst now tell him what "really happened." The analyst's experience is that he is now exerting, for him, maximum pressure for her either to acknowledge any murderousness in the situation as her own, or to disconfirm the internal seriousness of the situation by revealing her good-enough circumstantial explanation.

She says, "Let me think, because this is a precious example of what happens here and I don't want to squash it. I think where you may feel let down by me is that it seems I didn't have enough faith in you to expect that you would try to call back, enough to make extra sure the answering machine was on."

His response takes an unexpected turn, bringing in an aspect of the maternal relationship not put into words before. (Mother was previously seen primarily as narcissistically cold, manipulating admiration.) He says, "Yes . . . this is *like* mother, she always has this feeling I want to discard her, she feels all the men in her life want to discard her . . . she looks for examples and then flips into her killer mode, and it is going to be me who gets killed . . . that's how I felt as a kid, and it's how I still feel now. It's why I always feel I have to call her back immediately. . . . I read in the newspaper about a woman who killed her kid, that's how I felt as a kid, she had it in her to do that . . . and in the dream."

He is then able to offer further detail and associations about a dream element—leading unexpectedly to recalling a movie scene which had fascinated him in childhood, and going on to an elaboration of the movie in a passionate fantasy in the session. The fantasy involves a son sacrificed by his mother. It sounds as if it might correspond to a core masochistic latency fantasy. At any rate it is a memorable appearance of the motif of sacrifice, which becomes understandable and meaningful later in the analysis.[4] Following this session, the analysis becomes more collaborative. The analyst feels heightened interest and respect for the patient. The patient spontaneously becomes more reflective and curious about his early experiences with "the principal women in my life," and "how they have shaped me." I think we can take this an indicator that he is beginning to see transference as transference. He is now more able to confide the intensity of his prior chronic anxiety during sessions that the analyst would actually rape or kill him.

At the fourth sampling, the patient, during a session, spontaneously recovers hitherto repressed memories of dangerous sadomasochistic games played with a sibling throughout latency, in which the patient was in the role of "willing" sacrificial victim. It seems evident that the affects in these games were foreshadowed in the countertransference enactment five months earlier. The

[4]In earlier phases of the treatment this sadomasochistic fantasy appeared as a conviction that love required sacrifice, and though this conviction could be clarified, the treatment was experienced as a sacrificial ordeal, or the analyst was subtly threatened to see if she could be induced to sacrifice her personal time in the interest of more ideal appointment hours.

analyst surmises that the sadomasochistic relation with the sibling was heir to the sacrificial oedipal and preoedipal relationships.

Following this mutually satisfying piece of work, efforts to shift guilt, sadism, or passive wishes onto the analyst can be more readily caught, and more clearly seen by the analyst, and reproaches or pleas for a special idealized intimacy can be seen as defensive, and the patient himself begins to notice this. He undertakes a further exploration of the sadomasochistic modes of relating in his family and in himself, at this point with a more feelingful understanding of them as desperate ways to stay in contact.

Let us now look closer at the intervention "Why you feel let down is feeling I didn't have enough faith in you. . . ."

I propose this as an example of an intervention that successfully contains the projected guilt. It represents the analyst's containment of whatever provocative stimulations might otherwise eventuate in the analyst's subtly enacting the complementary role. In order to make this interpretation, in the pause to think, the analyst had to be able to tolerate and contain ambiguity in regard to guilt. That is, from different angles both she and the patient could be seen as partially implicated in aggressive acting out, even though the patient's fantasy that she had revengefully turned off the machine and walked out of the office wishing to kill him was not "true." She did not try to prove that the patient's projected or unacknowledged aggression was to blame. Nor did she accept omnipotent guilt for the mote in her eye, nor did she try to exculpate herself. This tolerance for the ambiguity evidently allowed her to move from a complementary identification (Racker, 1976) (being the patient's murderous object) to a concordant one (identifying with the patient's experience of unavailability as a meaningful, not accidental response to him).

In regard to the patient's response it is notable that he no longer pressed the analyst for what "really" happened. He is moved, perhaps by the affective rightness of the interpretation, to reflect on an experience with his mother. In this reflection he shows a nascent capacity to understand mother's point of view as well as his own (without being pulled into identificatory merger or compulsive reparations/reaction formations).

Could we consider this series of samplings as a kind of longitudinal section that could be made at various points in any analysis? Some of the aspects that interest me will be apparent from how I have made the cut: increased capacity for fantasy vs. concreteness, increased internal life vs. projections, etc. I would like to name one more: strain. Strain might be defined as the amount of work an analyst has to do at any given time not to be impeded by the countertransference. The counterpart of strain is resilience. In Winnicott's (1968) terms, resilience would be that "survival" of the analyst that makes him "usable."

A negative countertransference situation, elicited by a negative transference, for example, would indicate strain. It is not the negative countertransference itself that would be the strain but the degree of effort that must be made to understand and contain it without a retaliatory or defeated response, without mania or masochism, to use Racker's concepts (1976).

Jay Greenberg (1991) recently encouraged analysts to maintain "an openness to the patient's impressions (*of the analyst*) and an awareness of their plausibility, even when doing so gets uncomfortable" (p. 248). Discomfort is a part of what I am calling the strain factor. The above material could indeed be read as the story of how this particular analyst with this particular patient became more "comfortable" with the aspect of truth in the patient's perceptions. But such greater ease might sometimes have to be struggled for, or it too could be glib. I'd prefer to read this material as suggesting a parallel process in analyst and patient in terms of increased ability to experience internal reality. This would leave room to think of the analyst as accepting projections as well as accurate perceptions.

In conclusion, to return to the question of what is real: with regard to the intervention in the answering-machine episode, "Where you may feel let down . . ." we should note that the analyst does not take a position in regard to reality. She does not insist on whose reality should have higher priority. I think this is not just diffidence. More is involved here than even the fine notion of analytic tact (Poland, 1975). Not taking a position on reality makes it possible for both analyst and patient to shift from complementary to concordant identifications and back. It makes the possibility of multiple perspectives permissible and realizable.

Without claiming that this is the key mutative intervention, I would point out that it shows a way beyond the traumatic sadomasochistic relationship, a piece of which was that there was only one reality (S. Bach, personal communication).

REFERENCES

Greenberg, J. (1991). *Oedipus and Beyond.* Cambridge: Harvard Univ. Press.

Poland, W. S. (1975). Tact as a psychoanalytic function. *Internat. J. Psycho-Anal.,* 56:155–162.

Racker, H. (1976). *Transference and Counter-Transference.* New York: Int. Univ. Press.

Renik, O. (1993). Countertransference enactment and the psychoanalytic process. *Psychic Structure and Psychic Change: Essays in Honor of Robert S. Wallerstein, M.D.,* ed. M. Horowitz, O. Kernberg & E. Weinshel. Madison, CT: IUP.

Rosenfeld, H. (1987). *Impasse and Interpretation.* New York: Tavistock.

Sandler, J. (1976). Counter-transference and role-responsiveness. *Internat. Rev. Psycho-Anal.,* 3:43–47.

Winnicott, D. W. (1968). The use of an object. In: *Psycho-Analytic Explorations.* Cambridge: Harvard Univ. Press, 1989, pp. 218–227.

300 Central Park West
New York, NY 10024

Aspects of Reality, and the Focus of Interpretation

MICHAEL FELDMAN, F.R.C. Psych.

IN THIS PAPER I DISCUSS some of the difficulties associated with the notion of a dichotomy between physical and psychic reality, and the way in which the analyst's judgment concerning the nature of either influences his choice of interpretation. After briefly offering an alternative approach based on the concept of different *versions* of the history of physical reality and of psychic reality, I present clinical material to illustrate how the analyst may make use of information of different kinds—derived from his knowledge of the patient's history, his observations in the session of her tone and manner of speaking, as well as the contents of her material, and particularly his experience of the atmosphere and nature of the relationship that is being lived out between himself and the patient. Rather than trying to determine the nature of the patient's psychic reality as distinct from the material reality, the analyst can recognize, as the session unfolds, different versions of reality and can begin to build up a picture of that version which is most clearly manifested in the consulting room at the time, and which is probably the most useful focus for our understanding and our interpretive efforts.

Freud's delineation of the concept of psychic reality represented an important conceptual advance: "It remains a fact that the patient has created these phantasies for himself, and this fact is of scarcely less importance for his neurosis than if he had really

Michael Feldman is a Consultant Psychotherapist at the Maudsley Hospital, London; he is also a Training Analyst, British Psychoanalytic Society.

experienced what the phantasies contain. The phantasies possess *psychical* as contrasted with *material* reality, and we gradually learn to understand that *in the world of the neurosis it is psychical reality which is the decisive kind*" (1916–1917, p. 368).

This formulation may lead the analyst to try to discover the nature of the patient's psychical reality, to contrast it with the view of material reality he has arrived at. The analyst derives the latter from the history, his own observations, and constructions. He derives the former from the evidence of the patient's unconscious wishes and fantasies, as manifested in verbal material, behavior, dreams, and the wishes and anxieties that arise in the transference. The patient and the analyst may arrive at common convictions regarding the nature of this "reality," or they may develop different sets of convictions.

Bion (1963) has given a vivid illustration of the complexity of the relationship that may exist. He described a patient who reported a dream, which led the analyst to believe that the patient had had a dream. The patient, however, did not believe that he had had a dream but that he was giving a straightforward recital of a horrifying experience. He expected that, if he reported it as a dream requiring interpretation the analyst would confirm his daydream that it was only a dream, thus keeping at bay his conviction that the dream not only had been, but was still the reality of his experience.

The pressure on the analyst to make these distinctions derives not only from his own interest and curiosity and his more theoretical views of the requirements of the analytic process; it may also reflect the anxieties, uncertainty, or confusion aroused by the material the patient has brought, and the emotional impact of the unconscious currents present in the session, such as the one just described.

There will of course often be conscious or unconscious demands from the patient to attend to the "reality" of the situation, and it is vital for the patient to have a sense that the analyst is open to the realities of his current life, or his history, and the ways he is affected by the analytic setting. It is inevitable that the analyst will become drawn into having opinions, making judgments, apportioning responsibility or blame, basing these on his own experience and bias and on what he judges to be the "reality" of the situations with which he is presented. These forces may result in both patient and analyst becoming apparently quite reasonably concerned with facts, and history, with what the mother or father or partner was *actually* like, how they interacted with the patient, and with what effect. There will be similar concerns about the analyst's personality, technique, and conduct, and how these affect the patient.

The focus of the analyst's attention often *does* become drawn toward making judgments about either material reality or the patient's psychic reality—trying to assess, for example whether the patient's mother was *actually* cruel, whether she behaved in a seductive or intrusive fashion on a particular occasion. In that frame of mind, it is often difficult to attend closely to the reality of what is being enacted between the analyst and patient: the way the patient might be using the communication about his mother to subtly draw the analyst into an alliance with him against the mother or drive the analyst into an alliance with the mother against him, thus seeking to re-create important aspects of the oedipal configuration that exist in his internal world.

I am suggesting that the effective functioning of the analytic process depends, in part, on the analyst's capacity to recognize and to tolerate some of these pressures, to avoid forming premature (and often defensive) judgments concerning the nature of the patient's psychic reality or his material reality which have not emerged out of an understanding of the situation that is lived out in the analytic relationship.

In any case, the notion of a unitary "reality" may in itself be a defensive oversimplification, and we may have to tolerate the discomfort and uncertainty connected with the idea of different, co-existing "versions" of psychic reality, of material reality, and of history. In his account of fetishism, Freud (1940, p. 204) refers to "incomplete attempts at detachment from reality." This may result in two versions of psychic reality co-existing in the patient. There may be one, for example, based on his perception that the woman does not have a penis, the other based on the disavowal of such a perception.

In studying the complex relationship to reality in neurosis and psychosis, Freud (1924) suggested that although the distinction was not absolute, and the processes involved not completely successful, in psychosis there was an attempt to create a new reality in place of an unbearable old one. In neurosis, on the other hand, the subject creates "a *world of phantasy* . . . a domain which became separated from the real external world . . . kept free from the demands of the exigencies of life, like a kind of 'reservation'; it is not inaccessible to the ego, but is only loosely attached to it" (p. 187).

Money-Kyrle (1968, 1971) further explored the individual's relationship to psychic reality. He pointed out the distinction, on the one hand, between our capacity to discover the truth, when our perceptions and understanding of "the essential facts of life" correspond with some innately predetermined concepts (or class notions) and on the other hand, the distortions, misconceptions, or delusions which our emotional needs may give rise to. "Among the many innate preconceptions we may be endowed with, two are of particular analytic importance: the good breast, and the good creative intercourse." They are of particular importance because there are such emotional obstacles to establishing the corresponding concepts. The child may, instead, create a *misconception* either of the nature of the parental intercourse, or the source of goodness on which he depends (the mother's breast). Instead, "an object falsely recognised as the lost good object comes into being as the apparent object of desire" (1971, pp. 105–106).

Britton (1992, p. 4) describes how the individual may be driven to deny the painful and threatening reality of the parental sexual relationship. "If this denial threatens to sever the individual's hold on reality, then the Oedipal romance may be preserved, by splitting it off into an area of thinking protected from reality and preserved, as Freud described, like Indians in a reservation. This reservation, which may be an area of day-dream or masturbatory fantasy, can become the place where some people spend most of their lives, in which case their external relationships are only used to enact these dramas to give a spurious claim of reality to their fantasies which lack 'psychic reality.' In other people the reservation may be preserved as an island of activity, such as a perversion, separated from the mainstream of the individual's life."

Schafer (1983) has taken this argument further, suggesting that the positivistic model, where "Reality is 'out there' or 'in there' in the inner world, existing as a knowable, certifiable essence" is unsatisfactory. He maintains that the "epistemological assumptions inherent in psychoanalytic inquiry limit us always to dealing with *versions* of reality." We define situations and invest events with multiple meanings, and we are limited to "constructing some version or some vision of the subject in the world" (p. 234).

We need not adopt a purely relativistic approach to the idea of psychic reality, however. Money-Kyrle suggests there are concepts which are experienced as "true" by virtue of their relationship to certain innately predetermined concepts. Bion was also concerned with the relation between truth and psychic reality. He suggested that a sense of truth depended on the convergence of different "emotional views" of an object, derived from a variety of sources, and viewed from a variety of perspectives. "A similar correlation, made possible by bringing conscious and unconscious to bear on the phenomena of the consulting room, gives to psycho-analytic objects a reality that is quite unmistakable" (Bion, 1962, p. 310).

In the consulting room we may aim to facilitate the convergence not only of aspects of the patient's internal and external reality, with different "emotional views" of the transference object present, but the convergence between the experience of the patient and the analyst in relation to the phenomena that are being lived out, which lend the experience a particular sense of "truth."

Recent developments in our understanding of the mechanism of projective identification provide a further reason why the distinction between reality and fantasy in the analytic relationship may be difficult to maintain (Klein, 1946, 1952; Bion, 1957, 1959, 1962; Joseph, 1987; Rosenfeld, 1987). Insofar as this mechanism results in the object's coming to contain projected parts of the self, the patient's *reality* is that the object is *identified* with such projected elements. It has become increasingly apparent that this mechanism not only influences the patient's perception of *reality* in relation to the analyst, but that the subtle unconscious projections may have a real and direct effect on the analyst's affective state, his thoughts and actions (Sandler & Sandler, 1978; Ogden, 1979; Joseph, 1987, 198; Sandler, 1987).

In other words, the patient's "illusions," based on the complex interplay of experience and fantasy, manifest themselves not only in the patient's material, his perceptions and reactions, but also in their influence on the analyst and the analytic relationship. These phenomena, which are important means by which the analyst comes to understand the nature of the patient's internal object relationships, point to the fascinating complexity of the relationship between fantasy and reality in the transference.

The analyst's actual involvement in the transference-countertransference interaction in the consulting room offers him a unique means of access to the significant and vivid aspects of the patient's psychic reality enacted there. As Freud (1912) pointed out in a well-known passage, "This struggle between the doctor and the patient, between intellect and instinctual life, between understanding and seeking to act, is played out almost exclusively in the phenomena of transference. It is on that field that the victory must be won. . . . It cannot be disputed that controlling the phenomena of transference presents the psycho-analyst with the greatest difficulties. But it should not be forgotten that it is precisely they that do us the inestimable service of making the patient's hidden and forgotten erotic impulses immediate and manifest. For when all is said and done, it is impossible to destroy anyone *in absentia* or *in effigie*" (p. 108).

We might similarly argue that only on the field of the transference (and, one might add, the countertransference) can the analyst gain access to those aspects of the patient's psychic life which demonstrate their presence and force by manifesting themselves in the patient's object relations. He is otherwise forced to make judgments about them in absentia.

Schafer (1983, p. 124) describes the development, in the transference, of "a shared reality . . . in which new transference interpretations, jointly developed, stated by the analyst and uniquely modified by the analysand, become the basis of enriched, intensified modes of constituting experience in the life of the analysand. . . . The major transference phenomena represent the achievement of such simplified, focused ways of defining and acting within the analytic relationship that there can be no mistaking their meanings or avoiding their emotional manifestations or implications."

Joseph (1985, p. 448) stresses that transference is a living, changing set of relationships to which the patient brings the patterns of unconscious fantasy, impulse, conflict, and defense that constitute his psychic life. She suggests that it is important to get the patient's underlying assumptions into the open, for he often communicates his problems and lives out his early history in ways that are beyond his individual associations and beyond what he can express in words. "Interpretation dealing only with the individual associations would touch only the adult part of the personality, while the part that is really needing to be understood is communicated through the pressures brought to bear on the analyst." We may be able to capture these experiences which are "beyond words" only through the reactions and feelings the patient unconsciously attempts to arouse in the analyst. Joseph regards the subtle and complex ways in which the patient acts out in the session as our richest source of information about his internal world, his object relationships, and his history.

As Freud was aware, however, this approach also involves the analyst in a difficult and stressful process. The intensity of the work, the particular demands on his attention which flow from having to recognize and try to think about intense emotional experiences in which he or she is directly involved, with all the anxieties this arouses, may reinforce an approach in which the analyst defensively turns toward a more detached view of the nature of the patient's psychic reality, or material reality.

The *analyst's* version of the reality that exists between himself and the patient will, of course, not only be determined by his own perceptions, judgment, and theories, but influenced by his own anxieties and needs, which manifest themselves as his own fantasies concerning the relationship between himself and his patient. One of the difficult but essential tasks he is faced with is trying to gain some awareness of his own assumptions, which may carry the force of "reality," and furthermore to try to differentiate those elements which belong predominantly to himself from those which have been significantly determined by the patient's projections.

In trying to recognize and understand what is functionally most available and significant *for the patient* at that moment, and to frame an interpretation accordingly, I would suggest that the analyst's primary task is not to sort out the "reality" from the fantasy or distortions associated with any particular issue such as the patient's history or her experience of the weekend. It is rather to attempt to explore the *patient's* psychic reality as it is manifested in the analytical situation, which we assume reflects the significant and active dynamics of her internal world, and which it is essential to address in order to achieve psychic change.

The way the patient talks, the way she brings her problems, and what is evoked in the analyst, as well as the contents of her material, reflect vital aspects of the patient's internal reality. Naturally this latter arises both out of her early history and object relationships and her more recent experiences, including the ways in which the *analyst's* version of reality, how he communicates this, and how he behaves, impinge upon her.

In the transference and countertransference interaction we are inevitably confronted with the interaction of these different elements, thus gaining privileged access to the *reality* of the patient's internal world, rather than being forced to make judgments about the reality of experiences "in absentia." The impasse that may arise in the clinical situation, which may *appear* to revolve around the patient and analyst having different "versions" of the reality, say, of the patient's relationship with her parents, or some interaction in the analysis, may actually involve a quite different *kind* of issue. The patient may experience the analyst as having failed to recognize and understand some aspect of the reality of the patient's experience *in the analytical relationship.*

In the clinical material to follow, I illustrate the way in which it became possible to build up a picture of important, and what I believe were "truthful" elements of the patient's inner reality by focusing not only on her material but also on the way she communicated, its impact on the analyst, and the way he used his experience and understanding of this process in the choice and focus of his interpretations.

Patient's History

A young woman in her midtwenties whose father is connected with the Scottish aristocracy, spent her childhood living on a remote estate in the Highlands. She attended a small private school and was regarded as a model child. Her parents divorced during her early adolescence.

Considerable psychological disturbance was manifest both in her parent's generation and among her siblings. She describes her father as well meaning, but vague and unwilling or unable to confront any difficulties. She feels her mother is unable to engage properly with anyone. She often says the right things, but they seem to have no depth or meaning. The patient alternately feels deprived, bitter, and angry, sorry for her mother and protective of her or she becomes resigned to a view of the whole family as hopelessly damaged. During her adolescence she and a younger sister seem to have been considerably disturbed and very entangled with each other.

At the time of reporting, a difficult relationship with her boyfriend had recently ended, and he had abruptly moved out of the house they shared. The patient had used the links existing in her mind between myself and her boyfriend, Nigel, a young psychiatrist, to act out some of the fantasies associated with the analysis. Initially his functioning either as an ideal, gratifying parent or analyst, or a sister with whom she could "twin" was very gratifying. The entanglement with him and what he embodied for her led to intense possessiveness and jealousy, and subsequently to her feeling trapped in an intrusive and claustrophic situation with someone she couldn't get through to, and who didn't actually care about her; she felt driven to desperation and violence.

Clinical Material

The patient arrived for a Monday session a few minutes late, which was unusual. Her car had been damaged by a hit-and-run driver during a recent holiday, so she had been coming to her sessions by tube. She had told me about her car and assumed I knew she was traveling by public transport, but had never mentioned it. I noticed that she was breathless and dressed more smartly than usual.

After a few minutes she said that she felt strange being late. "I don't know why I can't just come in and say, 'I'm sorry I'm late,' in a normal way. It's odd, I've been taking the tube and can't get used to the idea that I can't control the tube. I can if I get there early enough. When I'm at home I don't ever think I'm going to be late, and when it comes to the five minutes when I should leave, I think it doesn't matter if I'm late. There is something very odd. In the beginning, when I started analysis, Nigel was always saying, 'You mustn't be late,' sort of joking about it. I feel angry about not having a car, I feel as if it is something Nigel has purposely taken away from me. All weekend, it hasn't been terrible or anything, but I felt really sad and hurt, and I found it difficult to work."

For the analyst, the reality of the situation included the impression the patient made when she arrived, and the way she began talking, in a rather fragmentary way, apparently quite self-absorbed, assuming him to be listening and following closely. Although many elements of what she said evoked thoughts, memories, associations, and speculations in the analyst, some of which were very familiar, the patient did not seem either to be fully engaged with what she was talking about, or with the analyst in the room with her. She communicated an expectation that the analyst would make some comments on what she had brought, in the usual fashion, *as if he understood something*. At the same time her tone and manner created an atmosphere in which it seemed that she had little belief that either of them would be able to make much sense or much use of what was happening.

In listening, the analyst is aware both of the communication of her actual loneliness over the weekend and the ways in which she misses Nigel, but he also makes assumptions about the implicit or unconscious references to another aspect of her "psychic reality," namely, the experience of her analyst not having been available to her over the weekend to tell her what to think and what to do. The convergence of these experiences left her feeling sad and deprived, on the one hand, and interfered with and robbed, on the other, so that she was unable to think or to work.

The analyst felt convinced, however, that if he were to articulate this interpretation, the patient would probably feel relieved that he had spoken, that he seemed to have been listening to her and sounded much as usual. She would almost certainly agree with such an interpretation, treating it as the sort of thing the analyst is interested in and often says, which usually has little or no impact on her.

What I am suggesting is that instead of focusing his attention on the patient's external reality or interpreting the possible references to the transference situation and its links with his knowledge of her history, it may be more valuable for the analyst to shift the focus of his attention to the impact of the patient's arrival, her mode of communication, as well as its contents, the responses these evoke in him, and his expectations about probable reactions to his interpretations. It may then become possibly gradually to develop a picture of two people, and their relationship compounded of both fantasy and reality that has a "presence" and hence a reality in the session. This might include, for example, a view of patient and analyst coming together under some pressure or urgency and becoming engaged in talking in a familiar and reassuring way, but which is actually a very odd sort of interchange in which nothing can really be understood between them.

There may then develop a creative dialogue in the analyst's mind, which the contents of the patient's material can illuminate, and help the analyst to orientate himself not only to the patient's experience outside the session, but to the difficulties manifest at that point *within the session*. Conversely, his awareness of the issues that become manifest in the transference situation, may also lend significance to her material, as when she refers to difficulties in communicating, and in finding a way of getting to her analysis, her dependence on her object, and her difficulty in working.

Of course the nature of the object relationship which manifests itself within the session has profound connections with the patient's early experience, her view of her parents, and more recently, the peculiar and unsatisfactory relationship that developed with Nigel, but these links were almost certainly not "real" for her at that point in the session, and it is very doubtful whether the analytic process would be advanced by trying to make them explicit. On the contrary, the analyst's experience with this patient in the past is that attempts at such explication often simply lead to the confirmation that nothing is being said that has much meaning, or is of much value.

The patient went on to tell me that over the weekend she had been speaking to a friend about Nigel. Her friend had criticized the way Nigel had treated her and gave her some news about his activities. The patient had asked her friend whether Nigel had inquired about *her*. The next night had been terrible: she had dreamt about him all night; they had split up, but he was talking in a warm and friendly way, saying he hoped they would get together again, although she didn't quite believe it.

The patient commented that she knew that she sounded really removed and distant. She paused and said she felt really angry with Nigel.

Once again it would seem as if the "reality" the patient was addressing is her preoccupation with Nigel—the criticism of the way he had treated her, his recent movements, whether he thought about her, and whether they might get together again. Her communication depended, of course, on her assumption that she was with an analyst who would listen, who was familiar with the issues she raised, and whom she hoped would respond in a warm and sympathetic way.

On the other hand, the *analyst's* reality included not only her description of her weekend experiences and the way she was speaking (which did indeed sound removed and distant) but his assumption that the patient was simultaneously communicating an important aspect of her unconscious reality, namely, her analyst's neglect and bad treatment of her (especially over the weekend), her preoccupation with finding out about his activities, and whether he kept her in mind. Her nights (and her dreams) are filled with such preoccupations, the fear that the "splitting up" that has occurred is not simply for the weekend, but forever. However warm, friendly, and reassuring her object, she doubts that the contact (such as it was) can ever be restored.

It is thus possible to construe the patient's references to Nigel as manifestations of her experience of having been abandoned over the weekend by a neglectful, hurtful analyst, split off and projected into Nigel, and to interpret this to the patient as an expression of an important current aspect of her psychic reality. Such a link might strike the analyst as very real and obvious, and the patient may (consciously or unconsciously) expect some interpretation along these lines. As I have suggested, such an approach to the exploration and interpretation of the patient's psychic reality *may* involve the analyst in making judgments about the meaning and significance of the references in the patient's material, which it could be useful to articulate in an interpretation.

The alternative is to use the interaction between the analyst's experience of the impact of the present reality of the clinical situation, and the material the patient brings, to build up a picture of the patient's experience of her objects and her relationship to them.

Returning to the session I have been describing, when the analyst did *not* respond to what she had said, perhaps by making rather predictable comments "in parallel" with her references to Nigel, her awareness of the reality of being in the session with the analyst was made apparent by her comment that she knew she sounded removed and distant. The disturbance caused by her experience of the analyst's silence was, however, immediately presented as her anger with Nigel, What gradually began to emerge in the tone as well as the content of her communication, as the session went on, was that she not only felt treated in a cruel and neglectful manner but believed that the underlying *reason* for her abandonment was that there was something profoundly wrong with her, and this led to the other person's giving up hope, and turning away.

She went on to say that she thought Nigel's friends had always wondered why they were together—he was so much more intelligent, well read and knowledgeable than herself. She had always felt that they deceived each other—he liked her on account of the activities she was involved in when they met, which interested and impressed him, but she never really understood why he stayed with her. She also hadn't really understood why she was with him, though she knew she was attracted to the fact that he seemed so caring, and came from the same area as her mother. A friend had said the patient was like a young girl who had been swept off her feet.

She added with some intensity that she couldn't bear the way he had left, she couldn't get him out of her mind, she still expected him to telephone, all the time; it gets worse and worse. She said she had the awful feeling that he had suddenly moved out in order to save face with his friends and colleagues. It was all so controlled, so thought out. "I feel it's so sick, all this holding back, being controlled, being discreet."

Although the patient was ostensibly trying to clarify her

thoughts about the relationship with Nigel, while listening to her material, the *analyst* was aware of the fact that she had often raised the question of why she had been taken as a patient, whether the analyst had been deceived, or seduced into thinking she was more attractive and interesting and less disturbed than she was. She also felt that her intense need to find someone, and somewhere she could be looked after made her very susceptible to being persuaded into something or "swept off her feet." The analyst could thus have decided to address his interpretations either to the "reality" of her relationship with Nigel, or his construction of the "reality" of her transference relationship to himself, *based on what she had said about Nigel,* or he could have made a complex interpretation that linked the two.

However, in attending to what seemed to be taking place at that moment in the session, the present reality the analyst felt he was encountering was the patient's increasing sense of desperation over his silence, her worry about what was going on in his mind, and her frustration and fury about what she construed as his holding back, being so controlled or discreet. The more she became aware of his silence, the more she feared that he could do nothing with her broken-up and distant way of thinking and talking, and had withdrawn in hopelessness. There was a considerable pressure on the analyst to speak, because until he did so she couldn't make sense of what was going on in her own mind and became increasingly desperate.

I decided at that point to interpret what seemed *to me* to be the most pressing aspect of her psychic reality, although I was not sure to what extent this was accessible to her. I said I thought that in the silence she felt deprived of any way of knowing what was going on in *my* mind, and this made it very difficult for her. Her involvement with Nigel had not only given her access to what he was thinking and feeling, but indirectly to what she believed went on in me, and this had enabled her to feel less anxious and uncertain about herself. Today, after the weekend, with no access to Nigel, confronted by my silence, I though *she* found it very difficult to work out what was happening, and I thought this stirred up her fears that I too might not be able to do anything with what she had brought, and that my silence might signify my hopelessness about her. I thought she then became very resentful when I did not rescue her from this anxiety quickly enough, by saying something.

She said yes, she thought Nigel did provide everything. Yesterday she was reading—it's not that she feels unintelligent, but she just can't retain things. She thought Nigel was so good at that, he had such a wealth of experience, he could talk about things in an interesting and informative way.

I interpreted that, while she confirmed how much she relied on Nigel to provide for her, she then demonstrated how much she actually left up to me. I had to be able to retain things, to think in a way she seemed unable to do, to make connections, and talk in an interesting and informative way, as I had done when I suggested that when there was a break, because she couldn't retain things for herself, she felt deprived of access to my mind, and through that, some sense also of what was going on in her.

She said, "It's funny, there is something I notice more and more with my family. I was talking on the telephone to my sister Catherine. She had been talking about suicide and said something about the marks she had made on her wrists, but yesterday she sounded O.K. I said, 'So you're not thinking about suicide?'—trying to continue from the previous conversation, and taking it seriously. She said, 'I know I would *never* do that, I'm too frightened.' " The patient went on to say that she knew that that was so; things often go without saying, like her assumption that I knew she had been coming by tube, or when she said, "I'm sorry I'm late." A lot of the time she thought I knew, or she assumed I knew. She added, "It's a funny thing with Nigel. With you I think it works, with Nigel, a lot of the time I presumed he knew, and he didn't."

While it seemed as if the patient's response had only very tenuous links to the content of the interpretation, and her reality remained largely oriented toward the conversation with her sister, it allowed the analyst to build up a clearer sense of the nature of the object relationship not only with her sister and Nigel, but with what was present and real at that moment in the consulting room. Her response, her way of talking as well as its contents, conveyed a vivid and desperate sense that she had little or no belief in the way one person tried sensibly and reasonably to remember and talk about the other's problems or disturbance. On the contrary, it was as if the only form of communication relied on "assumptions" or "presumptions," by which I thought she was referring to processes of getting into or being in the other person's mind in peculiar and intense ways, which became clarified and more explicit in the next session. Although the reference to suicide was apparently not meant to be taken seriously, in the atmosphere of *this session* it gave a hint of an underlying hopelessness that was very "real."

The patient began the next session saying that she had had a really disturbed night, she had been dreaming a lot. She had been upset the previous evening, thinking about her parents and the rest of the family. None of them have friends, people they continue to have a relationship with. When they lived in Scotland, they used to invite people from the neighboring estates once a year. Mother *always* baked a quiche. Mother had a friend for a while, but then she moved to Australia.

She went on, "I really got upset yesterday, I hadn't mentioned about going on the tube, thinking of the way I don't tell you about things, and lots of things I don't know how to do; maybe it takes time, and I will have to learn."

The patient brings her disturbing awareness that there is something strange, and different, not only about herself, but about all the members of her family. There was something appalling and desperate, particularly in her portrayal of her mother. She then refers once again to her own problems in knowing how to do things, how to communicate with me, and she offers the hope that in time she might learn such things, rather than be faced with a much more frightening and hopeless view of herself. However, her concerns about herself and her way of functioning seemed more available and more part of her experience of "reality." She seemed able to articulate this more clearly, and there was a sense in which her reality and the analyst's coincided more closely than in the previous session.

She then said, "I had this dream; I caught a kind of cold last night. In the dream I was seeing this woman, she was young and naked, and I was really attracted to her breasts. I wanted to touch her, and I was thinking—it's disgusting—that I would make love to her breasts and they would come inside my vagina. And then I thought maybe I see breasts as some kind of penis—I was a bit disgusted. I felt really warm and happy about this woman's breasts, they would take care of me. The idea of a penis is the complete opposite. It required much more out of me."

She was silent for a while, and then said, "You know I don't know what to talk about—I don't have the ability to decide what's important. I haven't any idea or pattern to know how I can say the things that are important."

I thought the dream could be understood not only as the patient's recollection of an illusory and transient event of the previous night, but as serving other "real" functions. First, as an (unconscious) commentary on her difficulty in talking directly to me, relating to me as she assumed other patients did. I took her dream as a description of an (illusory) world in which there are warm and caring breasts she can touch, which feed her and fill her vagina; she had no need to talk or to explain anything. In *dreaming* it she had withdrawn into this world, and in the session, I thought her narrating the dream the way she did, also served as a refuge from the painful and hopeless thoughts and feelings she had begun with. Being very conscious of my presence, and an expectation that she should make some comment about the dream, she tried to engage me by fitting in with what she sometimes assumed to be my ways of thinking and talking ("Maybe I see breasts as some kind of penis"). This felt quite unreal (to both of us, I think), and indeed I thought she was both bringing, and enacting an infantile fantasy which seemed to have little to do with adult sexuality.

While there was a greater sense of a shared reality in the room as, for example, when she said with some urgency that she didn't know what was important or what to talk about, there was also a powerful and real pressure on me to live out the dream with her *in the session*—to become the woman who offers her a direct means of bridging the gap between us, and filling the spaces inside her. The patient has described how she often just likes me to talk, she could just lie on the couch, as if cradled or rocked, not wishing me to stop. This defended her against a sense of need, of loneliness and anxiety, and also against having to be concerned about her state of mind, and what she felt was wrong with her, which she could only bear facing very briefly. When I didn't quickly respond to her invitation to *become* the object, or part-object in the dream, she began to panic, feeling she didn't know how to think, what to say, or where to go.

After a silence she continued, "Last night I felt really awful. I kept thinking I can't take that feeling anywhere, I can't come here, I felt there was no one to just look after me, to say, 'There, there.' I thought if you did just try to comfort me, that wouldn't work, I wouldn't be comforted—it wouldn't seem real, or a relief. I feel I'm just getting really ill now."

She paused and then said, "I mean I felt all over the place. I feel upset about what's happened and feel awfully alone and can't make it better. I feel I am incapable of making friends, and will never be able to. It's not that I think people don't like me; they do; it's just something about what I do that feels wrong, and I can't make contact. I feel so awful about my family. It is as if we are all yearning to make contact with other people or ourselves, but none of us is capable of it. I feel I ought to be more constructive here, but I feel I don't know how to do it."

I interpreted that she seemed to be very aware of something painful and disturbing. Like her mother and others in her family, she had a yearning to establish proper contact with friends, or to talk to me in an ordinary, straightforward way. When she tried to do this, however, she became desperately worried that for her, like her family, this didn't seem to work, it gave her little satisfaction, and she was afraid that no one could provide what she needed. She could have a *dream* about what would cure her feeling of cold: the woman's breasts she could look at, touch, or have inside her vagina and make her feel warm and happy and taken care of. Her worry in the actual session is that I made demands on her, like she said about the penis, and that wasn't any good. On the other hand, if I say, "There, there," and pretend to be a woman with breasts, it is very appealing, but would not feel real.

After a short silence she said, "You see I just don't know what I think I want. I don't know what other people get out of relationships. I really don't know how to look at it. I bumped into Laura and we went and had coffee together. I felt so awful, it was difficult to be with her. I asked her what she was doing, and she told me. It's not that I wasn't interested, but after a while, she said, 'Are you O.K.? You're not, and I'm babbling.' I said I was afraid of being extremely demanding of her or anyone else. Laura is being so nice to me. I'm not straightforward. I feel there is something about the way I complain or cry, which is incredibly demanding. Other people just cry or complain in an ordinary way. I really want to be able to have friends, to be a friend to people. I don't know why I can't. I don't know why I can't put something aside."

I said I thought she did know something of the reason. She did want to engage in an ordinary friendly way with Laura, but became aware of something different and worrying about herself that interfered with this, such as her uncomfortable awareness of the preoccupations and needs that she encountered in her dream. I thought she had a very similar worry in the session at the moment: she had found it very hard to listen to what I was saying, hard to do anything with it, and was frightened of being very demanding in a way I might not be able to stand.

The patient responded: "It's very odd, I feel in such a catch-22. The only way I feel something can be experienced is by you expressing it by *not* understanding, by turning up late, or not turning up at all one day. I felt what you said sounded exactly right, but it makes me feel sort of worried, and guilty. I don't know how I would ever—the only way I could ever express how I feel is like what my sister and I do together, like saying we were going to commit suicide, or the fights I had with Nigel, but of course that doesn't really work."

I felt that now there was much better contact between the patient and myself. She indicated that she could sometimes understand and agree with my interpretations, and I thought we were now both addressing something that seemed real and present but disturbing. And yet what had emerged was a clearer picture of the patient's despair about ever being able to engage in an "ordinary" way, like other people, to make use of words and "understanding" in a way that had meaning for her and offered any real help. She contrasted this with a much more concrete, primitive way of communicating—by talk about suicide, fights, or by the type of physical relationship with the breast she had dreamt about. She linked her disability, which she saw as serious and sometimes felt hopeless about, with the strange and disturbed qualities she encountered in different members of her family, especially her mother. It was clear to both of us that she often felt driven, rather frantically to *attempt* to engage in the way she saw other people doing—like her mother entertaining the neighbors with a quiche every year, but it felt unreal and unsatisfying to her.

Discussion

In this paper I have briefly touched on the theoretical and clinical difficulties that arise when attempting to discriminate between psychic reality and external reality. For both the patient and the analyst the present reality results from a complex interaction of elements of fantasy and experience, of mechanisms of projection and introjection. The analyst's task can be construed in terms of the recognition and understanding of crucial elements of the patient's inner world as they are presented and enacted in the analytic sessions. The pressures from the patient and the analyst's own defensive needs may lead him to focus his thinking or his interpretations on the "realities" of the patient's external life, or may lead him to make premature links between her relationship with the analyst as a whole-object transference figure, and aspects of her history and her external life. To the extent that it is possible to recognize and resist such pressures, the analyst may be able to remain in touch with the "actuality" of what is going on between them as the session unfolds and may come to understand how the patient's inner world is reflected in this interaction.

There are, of course, considerable difficulties in achieving this understanding. When, in this clinical example, the patient arrived for the first session and spoke about her anger, pain, resentment and jealousy in relation to a boy-friend who had abandoned her, the analyst had no reason to doubt the reality of this, but he was also inclined to assume that she was alluding to another aspect of her psychic reality, namely, the experience of having been abandoned *by him* over the preceding weekend. He was also aware of the way in which both of these experiences related to the patient's early history.

However, as he attended to the way the patient was talking and what she was saying, what became most palpable was the difficult, rather broken-up and detached way she had been speaking, her concern that she couldn't think or properly understanding what was going on, and her fear that the analyst's initial silence not only felt like an abandonment but arose out of his hopelessness about her.

In the course of the extracts from the two sessions I have described, it became possible to address with the patient the reality of her repeated experience of feeling herself to be "odd," strange, or different, like other members of her family—apparently able to engage in ordinary exchanges, but never feeling properly understood or able to understand the other person. The dream she reported in the second session, as well as the references to the talk about suicide, or fights with her boy-friend, indicated the extent to which she relied on very concrete, primitive methods of interacting—often with part- rather than whole-objects, to achieve any sense of satisfaction, however transitory.

I suggested that there was a considerable pressure on the analyst to engage with her in a way that allowed her to use his presence, his words, and tone of voice in just this way, creating the "illusion" of a dialogue in which two people seem to be understanding each other. To the extent that this succeeded, it would represent the re-creation of the object relationships to which she was accustomed, and about which she felt so despairing.

By resisting this pressure to some extent and trying to wait until a clearer sense developed of what was being manifested *in the analytical relationship,* it then became possible to address this in a way which I believe felt more difficult, but more immediate and real to both patient and analyst. What emerged was a vivid sense of an object relationship in which the patient was aware of her profound difficulties in relating in an "ordinary" way, and where she felt that the other person either entered into an unreal, illusory dialogue with her or abandoned her out of hopelessness and despair. The paradox is that when this relationship became available to be looked at and thought about, rather than repetitively enacted, she seemed actually to be in better contact with both her own inner reality and with the analyst, and there seemed to be a greater sense of shared perceptions and understanding. The experience of "containment" that seemed to result was accompanied by what appeared to be a greater degree of integration, and capacity for thought and reflection, and the emergence of the possibility of a more hopeful type of object relationship.

REFERENCES

Bion, W. R. (1957). The differentiation of the psychotic from the non-psychotic personalities. *Internat. J. Psycho-Anal.*, 38:266–275.

_____ (1959). Attacks on linking. *Internat. J. Psycho-Anal.*, 40:308–315.

_____ (1962). A theory of thinking. *Internat. J. Psycho-Anal.*, 43:306–310.

_____ (1963). *Elements of Psychoanalysis.* New York: Basic Books.

Britton, R. (1992). The Oedipus situation and the depressive position. In: *Clinical Lectures on Klein and Bion,* ed. R. Anderson. London: Routledge, pp. 34–45.

Freud, S. (1912). The dynamics of transference. *S.E.*, 12.

_____ (1916–1917). Introductory lectures on psycho-analysis. *S.E.*, 16.

_____ (1924). The loss of reality in neurosis and psychosis. *S.E.*, 19.

_____ (1940). An outline of psycho-analysis. *S.E.*, 23.

Joseph, B. (1985). Transference: The total situation. *Internat. J. Psycho-Anal.*, 66:447–454.

_____ (1987). Projective identification: Some clinical aspects. In: *Projection, Identification, and Projective Identification,* ed. J. Sandler. Madison, CT: Int. Univ. Press, pp. 65–76.

_____ (1988). Object relations in clinical practice. *Psychoanal. Quart.*, 57:626–642.

Klein, M. (1946). Notes on some schizoid mechanisms. In: *The Writings of Melanie Klein, Vol. 3.* London: Hogarth Press, pp. 1–24.

_____ (1952). Some theoretical conclusions regarding the emotional life of the infant. In: *The Writings of Melanie Klein, Vol. 3.* London: Hogarth Press, pp. 61–93.

Money-Kyrle, R. E. (1968). Cognitive development. *Internat. J. Psycho-Anal.*, 49:691–698.

_____ (1971). The aims of psycho-analysis. *Internat. J. Psycho-Anal.*, 52:103–106.

Ogden, T. (1979). On projective identification. *Internat. J. Psycho-Anal.*, 60:357–373.

Rosenfeld, H. A. (1987). Projective identification in clinical practice. In: *Impasse and Interpretation.* London: Routledge, pp. 157–190.

Sandler, J. (1987). The concept of projective identification. In: *Projection, Identification, and Projective Identification.* Madison, CT: Int. Univ. Press, pp. 13–26.

_____ & Sandler, A. M. (1978). On the development of object relationships and affects. *Internat. J. Psycho-Anal.*, 59:285–296.

Schafer, R. (1983). *The Analytic Attitude.* New York: Basic Books.

5 Cholmely Crescent
London N6 5EZ
England

The Analyst's Experience in the Psychoanalytic Situation: A Continuum Between Objective and Subjective Reality

ALAN Z. SKOLNIKOFF, M.D.

TRADITIONALLY, WHEN WE HAVE DESCRIBED strong feelings in psychoanalysis or psychoanalytically oriented therapy, our reference has been to the patient's capacity to experience these emotions in relation to the analyst. In contrast, the more recent psychoanalytic literature (Schlesinger, 1981; Tyson, 1986; Skolnikoff, in press) has begun to focus on the complexities of the *analyst's* emotional experience with the patient. In the present paper, I offer an outline for a continuum between objective and subjective reality in the analyst's perception of the patient. Through clinical example, I will attempt to illustrate the complexity of the analyst's emotional reactions, their influence on and reflection of the analyst's (often unconscious) perception of the patient, and the therapeutic value of carefully studying these reactions.

If we begin with the assumption that the analyst is as much an emotional participant in the analytic process as is the patient, then the concept of psychic reality applies to the analyst's thoughts and behavior as well as to those of the patient. Our recognition of this expanded field will have consequences for our clinical theory and for analytic technique. For instance, we may no longer hold to a

---

Dr. Skolnikoff is Training and Supervising Analyst, San Francisco Psychoanalytic Institute. He is Associate Clinical Professor, University of California, San Francisco.

narrow definition of neutrality in which the analyst reacts cognitively to the patient's transferences. Rather, we must begin to acknowledge a more profound emotional reactivity in the analyst, one that reflects the complex, mutual involvement of analyst and patient in the analytic relationship.

Support for this view comes from many quarters. Tyson (1986) points to a broadening of the definition of countertransference. From Freud's earlier, narrow definition of an undesirable, unconscious reaction to the patient that should be eliminated by further psychoanalysis, we now recognize that our conscious, preconscious, and unconscious reactions to the patient are inevitable parts of the analytic process. Despite this more inclusive definition, I believe the extent of the analyst's emotional involvement with his patient is still underestimated. More often than not, the analyst is involved in fantasy in a multifaceted relationship that transcends the narrow confines of the analytic situation. To talk about these feelings only on a conscious-unconscious continuum artificially restricts the range of emotions at which we look. We would be better served to consider an objective-subjective continuum in the analyst's reactions as the relationship with the patient develops.

Perhaps it is the setting of the work that encourages such a mutual relationship. Two people meet alone behind closed doors four or five hours a week for several years. They cannot help but experience strong feelings and fantasies about one another. Although the analyst does not reveal his innermost feelings, he certainly is encouraged to be emotionally receptive to this patient to remain empathically involved. In fact, his not talking openly to the patient might stimulate in him more fantasies about his situation. This is not to negate the analyst's need and capacity to translate most of these thoughts into an understanding of the intrapsychic dynamics of the patient. He also studies his idiosyncratic responses to the patient as part of his continuing self-analysis.

The analyst's capacity for understanding his responses is often limited to retrospective observations as he gradually learns about the patient's dynamics. While we can view the psychoanalytic process as one in which the patient experiences transference wishes toward the analyst and attempts to observe them with the analyst's help, from a two-person perspective, the analyst also experiences emotional reactions toward the patient. And he attempts to observe these within himself in order to better understand the patient. Thus *both* patient and analyst remain emotionally engaged and simultaneously observe the nature of this engagement. This is a complicated task for both participants, since each will have difficulty experiencing and observing at the same time (Sterba, 1934). Although the analyst may follow the sequence of the patient's emotions, it may be difficult for him to simultaneously understand his own emotional reactions, particularly during the middle phase of the analysis when the patient and analyst may both experience strong transferences and so may not be able to maintain a clear, relatively unbiased view of the therapeutic process. It is in this "intersubjective realm" (Skolnikoff, in press) of mutual emotional involvement that subjective reality predominates for each member of the analytic pair.

Schlesinger (1981) describes one aspects of the analyst's subjective involvement as the empathic process. Here the analyst must steer between two poles. On the one hand he may be overinvolved and identified with the patient in attempting to understand him and feel empathetically, which could compromise his psychological objectivity. On the other hand, he might be excessively detached and feel alienated. Or one stance might defend against the other, as when an analyst might find himself feeling detached with a patient out of a need to control excessively erotic or aggressive emotional responses within himself.

A common dilemma can be seen when the patient wishes acknowledgment from the analyst of a real life event such as a birth, death, or other significant milestone. The analyst might try to get the patient to observe the meaning of the wish for acknowledgment. However, even if he theoretically believes he should avoid gratifying his patient, he might inadvertently indulge him with comments such as "How sad!" or "Congratulations!". He might note that on certain days a patient is exuberant and entertaining, and on others boring and off-putting. Other reactions might make the analyst angry or irritable. For example, he might have a negative reaction to the patient's sharp tone or an attitude he finds obnoxious. In terms of being empathically engaged, it is almost impossible to avoid feeling some emotional response as one actively listens. The analyst's work is of course to understand his reactions to the patient's productions and use them to understand the dynamics. But the act of understanding often leads to distance. Paradoxically, understanding and interpreting can lessen emotional involvement. The analyst often emotionally experiences the patient who is having strong transference reactions as bad—seductive or rejecting, boring or exciting. The analyst might react to his emotions either by looking forward to or dreading seeing the patient. Understanding and observing these feelings and interpreting them often returns the analytic pair to a more neutral, less subjective position.

Enactment is another term that some of us use to convey an aspect of the analyst's subjective involvement. Pick (1988) describes how the patient has a desire for an enacting response from the analyst. The analyst also has the impulse to enact, and this impulse is often expressed in the act of the interpretation. The enactment in the interpretation may express itself in several ways: implicit indulgence or caressing the patient with words; hostile or frozen responses that deprive the patient of what he yearns for. McLaughlin (1991) talks about "enactment" as different from countertransference and projective identification. The patient behaves in a particular way to get a response from the analyst. The analyst in turn, because of his empathic attunement and/or unresolved conflicts, behaves in a way that "enacts" a sequence that elucidates the transference-countertransference.

When one considers the origin of the need to communicate within the mother-infant dyad, one can extrapolate similar considerations to the psychoanalytic situation. One of the analyst's primary functions is to listen quietly, taking in what the patient is saying, which in itself satisfies the patient's yearning to be heard. The experience of the mother who feeds her child, with the child opening his mouth in response to the mother's offering food, leads to the mother's responsively opening her mouth as she feeds the child. This involuntary response can be seen as the root of empathy—the oral pleasure that the mother has in identifying with her child's gratification. In contrast, the child who rejects the food that is offered often elicits a "clenched teeth" response from the mother.

In the psychoanalytic situation, the analyst may feel gratified or rejected, depending on how the patient responds to his interventions. There are compliant patients who indiscriminately take in whatever is offered. Others feel they must respond positively to whatever is offered lest the analyst feel rejected, diminishing his capacity to give further "nourishing" interpretations. It is important to recognize the continuing mutual responsiveness that characterizes the everyday, usual analytic behavior of the analyst-patient pair.

To what extent does the analyst's language merge with that of the patient? Empathic communication might imply that the analyst attempt to use the patient's language in his interventions. This practice, in a setting in which analyst and patient feel attuned to or identified with one another, might lead to some confusion. The patient and analyst might not be clear about the origin of a particular interpretation. The patient may give the analyst information with an unconscious wish that the analyst give it back in the form of an interpretation. The childhood-feeding metaphor would be: the child gives the mother the food to feed him. In the psychoanalytic situation, this is not always a fantasy. The interpretation, "You have the impression that this is your idea rather than mine because you can't accept it as coming from me," could be said by either patient or analyst.

Beyond words, there are paralinguistic considerations such as voice tone, background noises, and the psychoanalytic ambiance that influence perceptions. In case presentations, or even in self-reflection, it is difficult to reproduce the context of the work unless all of these details are included. The analyst's subjective distortion must also be taken into account.

During the consultation process and the early portions of the opening phase, objective reality predominates. Transference and countertransference potentials tend to be preconscious. The analyst expects that his interventions will have single meanings and be so understood. As the opening phase progresses and the analyst becomes more emotionally engaged with the patient, objective reality becomes admixed with subjective impressions. The analyst begins to become aware of the development of more elaborate, preconscious countertransference attitudes in response to the patient's transferences, as well as to conscious conflicts within himself. During this phase, the analyst attempts to use the language of the patient to create an ambiance that is congenial for the work.

In the middle phase, a sense of confusion about the emotional interaction may develop and persist for longer periods, as objective reality alternates with subjective reality. Now countertransference may become less patent, with the analyst unaware of certain attitudes or behavior, "blind spots," which must be inferred by self-reflection, self-analysis, or eventual consultation. It is a restrospective distortion to assume that the analyst is always working systematically and objectively in this middle phase. During this period, the analyst needs tolerance for puzzling affects and behaviors that he may feel toward his patient.

In termination and posttermination phases, we presume analyst and patient have a relatively clear perspective on what occurred during the analysis. This assumption, however, may be relative. Clinical experience demonstrates that the transference–countertransference sequences are often poorly understood or remembered by the patient or analyst.

The question may be raised, "How useful is it for the analyst to focus on his subjective reactions?" Will this not distract him from an objective study of the patient's conflicts and transferences? I think there is greater danger in the analyst being lulled into a false understanding of the patient because of his failure to observe the meaning of his own subjective reactions. The patient has the opportunity for a more genuine analytic experience with a thorough working through of his transference resistances and conflicts when the analyst's focus is on the "intersubjective realm."

Two clinical examples will illustrate some of what I have been describing. The first is from an enactment in a case described by Poland (1992), and the second, from an analysis I conducted 15 years ago, with some retrospective thoughts about my subjective involvement.

Let me start with an extract from Poland's case (p. 191).

> Although I do not answer the telephone during a patient's hour, one time I answered when Mrs. R was late and I thought it might be her call, explaining her absence. To my surprise, however, I heard a voice . . . speaking Italian, a language which

> I know not at all. I assumed it was a wrong connection, but in rapid and urgent tones the speaker repeatedly used my name. . . .
>
> I found myself feeling not as if I were at home in my own office but as if *I* were the one with a language problem, as if I were lost and alone in a country where I could not speak the language.
>
> It was just then that Ms. R walked in and found me looking confused and in need of rescue. And, just then, I remembered that Ms. R had lived for a year in Italy. I must have looked pathetic and perhaps even urgent as I held out the receiver for help.
>
> Ms. R took the phone, spoke briefly, hung up, and told me that the voice at the other end was someone who wanted to invite me to Milan and who would write the details. The entire incident, which occurred during the middle of Ms. R's third year of analysis, took only a minute or two, but it opened a world between Ms. R and me.

Poland goes on in the body of the article to describe at length and in convincing detail the patient's reaction to his having handed her the phone. He also offers an inference about his behavior. He states (p. 192) that she "tried very hard to be a proper analysand. . . . She had seemed wary of me and on guard against my spontaneous exposure of feelings concerning our interaction. At times I wondered whether something she said had in it extremely subtle implications of criticisms or, at other times, some extremely subtle implicit humor. But efforts to push the boundary to expose such possible implications had never succeeded."

This incident served as a turning point in the analysis, in which the patient was better able to reveal anger at certain traits in an imperious mother, and become aware of her identification with some of those traits. Poland is convincing in describing the strands of the transference and his reconstructions. He does not tell us what motivated his action toward the patient, saying only that it wasn't "good analytic technique."

I would venture to disagree. To my mind, Poland's gesture was the kind of spontaneous analytic behavior that frequently occurs in the middle phase of an analysis, where the analyst permits himself through his receptiveness to be subjectively involved. Although I cannot guess why Poland was motivated to do what he did, the incident does seem to be a general metaphor describing an analyst's plea for "translation and clarification" of the patient's deeper emotions. It is as if he is dramatically saying, "I can't understand—can you help me?" Nor did Poland offer information about his reactions to not understanding the conversation on the telephone and how that could have pertained to his work with the patient. We don't know Poland's experience of the patient but might speculate. Did the patient evoke a helpless feeling in him in a variety of ways leading to the telephone enactment? Perhaps Poland was aware of conflicts within himself as he continued to be frustrated by the patient's emotional distance that led him to feel an increasing helplessness. Did he make earlier attempts to clarify his reactions with her?

One speculation is that speaking on the telephone resembles the experience of speaking and listening for both patient and analyst in the analytic situation. Neither has visual contact with the face of the other. Handing the patient the telephone for her to translate a conversation that he could not understand was a dramatization of his difficulty understanding her. In the impromptu theater of role-playing with reversal of roles, he might have been asking, "You understand something about yourself which I can't translate. As you can see, I don't know Italian. Can you help me? If you can, then maybe you will realize that you can also tell me more about yourself." It seems to me that resistances in analysis are by their very nature frustrating, and we interpret patiently, waiting for our patients to relieve us of this frustration. Although Poland's action may not be designated "correct technique," it certainly *can* be described as a creative enactment leading to a weakening of the patient's resistance.

My own case is not so dramatic. I initially had difficulty maintaining an emotional involvement with a man with a heavily obsessional style. Serendipitiously, in the middle of the analysis, some unplanned interactions led me to develop strong feelings about him, and I found myself more subjectively involved. Although I had some rational understanding of why this subjective relationship developed, it continued to influence my behavior toward him throughout the analysis. The patient achieved some major beneficial changes in his life, despite my being unable to resolve my subjective attitudes.

He was a 36-year-old, single, professional man with varied business interests and successes. He complained that, although he enjoyed great success in his profession and business, he lacked enthusiasm for marriage and children, although that was what he thought he wanted. He felt successful with women, but saw himself as having an attenuated sex drive. He appeared interesting, psychologically minded, and sophisticated in his capacity to think in a variety of modes, including his business, profession, and general philosophy. In the consultation hours, it seemed clear he had serious oedipal conflicts. His mother favored him over an eccentric father. His neurotic depression was in identification with his less-favored younger sister and eccentric father, both of whom had depressive moods.

I recommended analysis, which he readily accepted. I was surprised at the extent to which I found him dull in the early analytic sessions. He spoke perfunctorily about business matters, his profession, and women. I confronted the patient about whether he knew how uninvolved he appeared to be. Did he think he was depressed? He said that was the way he was and did not understand what I was talking about. In response to his continued dull intoning, I found myself feeling sleepy in almost every hour. After a while I thought I hit upon a way of understanding the patient's productions. I assumed that he might be repeating a form of relatedness that he had in childhood toward his mother. Perhaps he related perfunctorily to defend against a wish for attention. Questions and comments along these lines did not help, but what seemed to engage him somewhat were my comments about his shifts in mood. I continued to be bored and wondered, over the course of the next year and a half, whether the treatment was going anywhere.

At that point an unexpected interaction occurred. On one occasion I used the word *labile*. The patient said he did not understand. I was surprised because I knew he was well educated. I explained the meaning, and he replied he was surprised that I used such a word and wondered if I was trying to tell him something. One thought that I did not reveal was that I might have been using "big words" to compete with and impress him. Perhaps he felt insulted that I had to tell him the meaning of a word that he should have already known. Somewhat later, a similar interaction occurred. In using the word *egregious* to describe his reactions to a business client, he pronounced the middle "e" as "a." In order to be sure I understood him correctly I asked, "Do you mean egregious?" He responded "yes," realizing that I was pointing out his mispronunciation. He did not seem to mind then, but the following day was annoyed about what he felt I had done to him. I was doing the same thing that his mother did. I was using big words that he did not understand and insulted him further by correcting his pronunciation. He hated it when his mother did this, and he did not like it when I did it either.

This intrigued me because it appeared to be the first evidence of a transference reaction. (Today I would call it an enactment, being more comfortable with the notion that the patient had evoked a warded-off identification in me which led me to correct him. I realized that this interaction made me feel more involved with him than I had been before.) I though that we had the beginning of a maternal transference, but what seemed more important in terms of a subjective relationship that was developing was that I saw the connection between his mother and mine. When I was an adolescent, my mother had also been critical of my vocabulary and pronunciation. But this is retrospective. Fifteen years ago, I thought I was more deeply involved because of my understanding of his transference. I did not really see my contribution to the development of the transference by my action. I began to hear the patient's dull renditions as a defense against my criticism. He continued to imagine that I was critical of him, although there was no further conscious provocation.

This understanding did not lead anywhere in the next few months, and the patient began to feel discouraged. Then he developed a fantasy that he had not had since early adolescence. At that time, after an altercation with his mother in which once again she criticized him for being impertinent and not doing his homework, he went to his room and lay listlessly on his bed. He entertained grandiose fantasies: If he studied hard he would be able to get away from home by going to an excellent university. Who knows, some day he might become President of the United

States. At that point, his thumb, which he held near his mouth as he was musing about these ideas, became numb and felt enlarged. Now, on the couch, as he mused about being unable to accomplish anything and remembered his adolescent experience, he suddenly had the same sensation around his thumb and mouth.

As part of my subjective relationship with the patient, I emotionally joined him in feeling criticized and retreating to his room. I remembered my own retreats from a critical mother and my grandiose fantasies of escape. My patient was now my soulmate. I would help him with his mother because it resonated with my own experience. Retrospectively, even though I might have been overidentified with him, my subjective relationship with the patient was useful in supplying the emotional energy necessary to listen to and be empathetic with his productions. Although I continued to maintain a capacity to be objective by recognizing my overidentification instead of acting it out, the energy that fueled my involvement was this subjective relationship.

Another feeling developed toward him, partly in response to his perception of me. In these situations, it is never clear who is feeling what or what is objective. In so subjective a situation the analyst or patient can project or introject what to an outside observer can be considered either fact or fantasy. I was taller and more athletic than the patient. The patient commented on this difference, presuming that I had more success with women and was confident about my appearance. I felt, in my subjective relationship with him, that his feeling was objective, and that I would help him overcome his insecurity about his appearance vis-à-vis appropriate women. Although I never directly coached or reassured him, I had the feeling that he understood my solicitous intentions. I felt that we colluded not to discuss this feeling we had about one another more directly, possibly because I felt nothing could be done about it or that it was not appropriate for my role. I also felt he might feel humiliated if I spoke of it. At that time I never saw my attitude as warding off my discomfort with his attachment to me.

In this context he spoke of being humiliated, feeling short and fat and not wanting to expose his body to a beautiful woman to whom he was attracted. In order to remain potent during sexual intercourse, he created a homosexual fantasy in which he imagined a tall, athletic man being sexually attracted to him. If he imagined this man caressing him or having anal sex with him, he felt more potent and could be a successful heterosexual performer. He was ashamed that he needed this fantasy to maintain his excitement. I felt that if I were to interpret that I was the tall, athletic person in his fantasy, I would humiliate him. Instead I made an extra-transference interpretation of his need for a tall, athletic man as someone he thought the woman would prefer.

Discussion of this need appeared to permit the patient to be able to find an appropriate woman. His sexual drive increased considerably, although he was left with some homosexual fantasies that troubled him. I tenuously tried but was unable to interpret these fantasies in terms of the transference. Although the patient was satisfied with the changes in his life, I was left with a feeling of an incomplete analysis because of my inability to interpret the warded-off homosexual transference. I also wondered whether my subjective relationship with him, which I could not completely analyze, was indirectly responsible for this failure. Was I unable to analyze my involvement insofar as I too much enjoyed his displacement of the tall, athletic man onto me, which perhaps defended us both against the transference image of the critical mother, a less appealing one for me and one that I defended against by feeling more comfortable with being just like him, the criticized son. Another possibility was my homophobic fear of a more intense homosexual transference, which made my interpretations awkward. These reflections were in retrospect.

Subsequently I discussed my relationship with this patient with a peer. He described similar experiences with passive male patients. He found himself reacting to their passitivity with boredom, sleepiness, or by reactively overinterpreting to stay alert. Talking with him stimulated me to rethink my activity with my patient and led me to some of the conclusions described above.

Discussion

What I have attempted to illustrate with this example are the complex determinants behind my failure to fully translate into objective interpretations some of the subjective thoughts that occurred to me during the analysis. Although at the time I felt I was able to maintain sufficient objectivity, retrospectively, I have come to feel that the work was altered, in part, by my overidentification with the patient in relation to his mother. And yet, paradoxically, the very overidentification that might have compromised some of my capacity to interpret his transferences, simultaneously fueled my interest in the patient and may even have been the main stimulus for the analytic work.

While there were many other complex countertransferences and enactments—e.g., at times, he drew me into enacting the role of the critical mother—what I wish to emphasize is my belief that most, if not all, analyses contain important enactments and transference-countertransference reactions that, at the time of their occurrence, are not completely understood. It is the continuing *attempt* to understand these interactions by both members of the analytic pair that may be related to positive changes in outcome.

I believe that the unconscious subjective reactions I have described are ubiquitous, and the analyst's eventual awareness of them leads to a richer unfolding of the analytic process, with the patient enabled to have a more profound transference experience. Further, there is less danger that the analyst will be distracted from the patient's dynamics by being aware of his subjective reactions than that he will overlook some intrapsychic dynamics of the patient. I recommend that whenever possible in case presentations, the analyst present these subjective reactions as a central part of his thinking about his patient.

REFERENCES

McLaughlin, J. T. (1991). Clinical and theoretical aspects of enactment. *J. Amer. Psychoanal. Assn.*, 39:595–614.

Pick, I. B. (1988). Working through in the countertransference. In: *Melanie Klein Today, Vol. 2,* ed. E. B. Spillius. New York: Routledge, pp. 34–47.

Poland, W. (1992). Transference: An original creation. *Psychoanal. Quart.*, 61:185–205.

Schlesinger, H. (1981). The process of empathic response. *Psychoanal. Inq.*, 1:393–416.

Skolnikoff, A. (in press). Paradox and ambiguity in reactions of the analyst at work. *Psychoanal. Inq.*

Sterba, R. (1934). The fate of the ego in analytic therapy. *Internat. J. Psycho-Anal.*, 15:117–124.
Tyson, R. (1986). Countertransference evolution in theory and practice. *J. Amer. Psychoanal. Assn.*, 34:251–274.

205 Edgewood Avenue
San Francisco, CA 94117

Structural Actualities of the Transference and Their Effects on the Analyst's Functions

STANLEY L. OLINICK, M.D.

COUNTERTRANSFERENCE IS NOT THE ONLY POSSIBLE determinant of an analyst's inept or erroneous responses, and surely not of his relevant responses to the patient. This is true whether countertransference is conceptualized in its classic sense, as interference with an orderly process or, more broadly, as a source of information about the patient. *An analyst's difficulties or his ease and accuracy of functioning may also follow from his or her reality-oriented response to actual, generic, structural attributes of the transference itself.* These structural actualities may impair the analyst's capacity for clinical inference and judgment. They can affect the seasoned analyst as well as the novice, and the consequences to the analyst's functions may contribute to inherent difficulties in the analytic situation. They may become manifest, for instance, in the analyst's relative or absolute failure promptly and accurately to recognize, integrate, and respond to the analytic data.

Structural Effects Distinguished from Countertransference Responses

By "structure," I refer to the familiar definition, "enduring processes or functions" (Rapaport, 1967). Structure, however, is a

Dr. Olinick is Clinical Professor of Psychiatry at Georgetown University School of Medicine.

heuristic, *ad hoc* conceptualization, a verbal convenience for discussion. The analyst actually confronts and works with the interactions and transactions of the patient's transference and other processes and functions through the medium of language and the patient's gestures and enactments. We observe among the communicative interactions between two persons the inductive effects of one person's affects on another's. The communicative effects of such affective ambiances constitute part of the actualities of the transference, automatically inducing responses within the interlocutor.

Structural actualities of transference are the expressions and derivatives of underlying conflictual defenses and compromises. They are represented in the following categories, each being part of a transference system with potential for inducing effects in the analyst that may interfere with his appropriate functioning but do not necessarily progress to the dysfunction of a countertransference.

(1) The multiple, often obscure and shifting *meanings* of the transference manifestations. This is one of the "givens" of transference, a frequent source of confusion and puzzlement to the analyst, interfering with his optimal functions of tracing meaning and communicating this in due course to the patient.

(2) Transference as *struggle or agon*. This develops when the analyst is unwillingly drawn into a struggle with the patient over any aspects of the ongoing work. It may in part be a consequence of the shifting meaning of the transference, often including the projective or externalizing manipulations resorted to by the patient in order to stabilize his transference resistance.

(3) The chronic affective mode or modes in which the transference may be expressed. Transference, with its *affective ambiance,* may be related to historically conditioned grievances, to a sadomasochistic orientation, or to other dynamics that entail a chronic mode of affect expression, tending to induce a corresponding affect in the analyst, but not inevitably proceeding to a transference-countertransference agon.

(4) The plausible but inauthentic and *dissembling behavior* by which transference may be expressed. Certain transference expressions, repetitions, wishes, and states may engender dissembling behavior in a patient, which misleads the analyst and causes a disruption in his analytic functioning.

(5) *Transference repetitions.* These are also a source of confusion and frustration that may interfere with the analyst's functioning. They are often linked with transferences driven by grievances or an angry nostalgia (Olinick, 1992).

(6) The *narcissistically motivated peremptoriness* of certain transference manifestations. The affective ambiance of certain expressions of transference may be associated with a narcissistically motivated peremptoriness that tends to subvert analytic interactions. Initial impressions of a transference resistance, especially of an enactment or acting out, are sometimes of their peremptory, dogmatic, defensively narcissistic quality. It is often suggestive of what, in actors' or other stage performances, we would term "presence," that which rivets the audience's attention and suspension of disbelief. I am not suggesting that this phenomenon is necessarily artificial, histrionic, or that it pertains to specific diagnostic groups. All of these effects are in part contingent upon the uniqueness of the analytic setting and situation, on the analyst's devoting himself to the process and to the patient's presentation, in this way opening himself to transference effects.

Each of the preceding items enumerated needs to be understood in the context of the analysand's conflictual defenses, their derivatives and expressions as these are organized or structured into transference as resistance. There is overlap at times with role responsiveness, in the sense formulated by Sandler (1976), as well as with countertransference in the classic senses of the term.

I submit these also as features to be included in a definition of transference. Each is prominent in transference as resistance; some will have been immediately recognizable with their naming. The list is not exhaustive and surely includes inescapable shadings of classification—e.g., affective ambiance is a function of character and is also a function of transference.

To distinguish between the patient's characterology and the transference is a daunting if not impossible task. In the course of the psychoanalytic process, these two phenomenologies blend, and distinctions become moot. Each is contingent upon the other to the extent that distinguishing features become irrelevant or hypothetical. The functions that I subsume under the heading of "actualities of transference" inevitably include characterological enhancements and accentuations that can be traced to the regressive dynamics of the transference; in fact, they constitute some of the material from which transference derives.

Any presentations from the patient may in fact evoke responses in the analyst; the structural actualities under review here—the "givens" of the transference—can be perceived by the analyst as regularly occurring, "impersonal" groups of functions that, so to say, "come with the territory." Their actualities are without symbolic or metaphoric meaning, though these may accrue secondarily.

I am anticipating the demurral that these features of the transference are in fact integral to any personality and to any interpersonal relationship; they are ubiquitous in human relatedness. Precisely so. Transference is not confined to the psychoanalytic situation, nor is it always pathological. Its presence is a factor in the conserving of the past of the individual and the group, and in placing the stamp of individual and familial uniqueness on the larger society.

Countertransference reactions differ from the phenomena I am designating in that they are usually more persistent, insistent, and discomforting. They tend to be retained as secrets from colleagues and supervisors. A rule of thumb to distinguish reactions to the structural actualities of transference from countertransference reactions is the presence of literalized metaphoric connections. By this I mean that in countertransference reactions, the patient is no longer solely the patient, but is now a partly fictionalized stand-in or representative for someone of historical importance to the analyst or for some aspect of the analyst himself. The "as if" or "play" quality of the analytic situation has changed from "this represents that" to "this *is* that." For instance, looking forward with eager pleasure to a patient's appointment is probably not a response solely to the structuring of that person's transference, though it might initially reflect the affective ambiance engendered by the patient. It warrants examination of the probability that in the analyst's eyes the patient is now representing something other than who he or she truly is. I say "something" rather than "somebody" because countertransference-motivated relations are to part-objects, further signifying that some aspect of the patient's and/or the analyst's self has become metaphorized by the analyst to suit his/her particular unconscious requirements.

Although these distinctions between regressive, literalized, metaphoric countertransference responses and the reality-bound responses to the structural actualities of transferences shade into each other, attention to these details is important. The successful delineation of these distinctions can also have the serendipitous effect of at least partly freeing the concept of empathy—an instrument of trial identification, of "feeling into" and thereby of understanding the patient in context—from its sequestering in a vaguely defined countertransference perceptivity on the analyst's part, the latter arising perhaps from some unconscious features shared by analyst and analysand. Consequently (though I am not naively sanguine about this) it may also free the term *countertransference* to return to its original sense of a counterreaction denoting unanalyzed residues in the analyst, rather than centering in an incompletely valid, indirect source of information about the analysand. The concept of structural actualities of transference reemphasizes clinical judgment and inference, rather than a rudimentary intuition.

Transference as Struggle: The Analyst Drawn into an Agon

While psychoanalysis is a causal, rational theory of therapy, in practice it involves tension, struggle, and oppositionalism. Intrapsychic struggle is projected, externalized, and displaced into the interpersonal field. These dyadic interactions are perhaps not often enough emphasized in our literature, particularly as to their potentially remedial and salutary effects which are beyond the scope of this paper (but see Bird, 1972; Olinick, 1989; Boesky, 1990).

I suggest *agon,* in its senses of contest, anguish, and drive, as a comprehensively descriptive term denoting an involvement by the analyst, though not always to the extreme of a countertransference. The effect is usually limited in extent and intensity, as for instance in the two vignettes to be cited. With variations and modifications, one may expect to encounter it at times in any analytic situation, the result of continuing exposure to the complex real affects projected, externalized, and displaced by transference.

The affective ambiance of the patient is one of the driving forces of the potential agon. A classic instance of this is discussed by Freud on transference love (1914), and I cite excerpts for illustration:

> . . . the state [of the patient's] being in love . . . in the course of analytic treatment has the character of a 'genuine' love. . . . Nevertheless, . . . certain features . . . ensure it a special position. In the first place, it is provoked by the analytic situation; secondly, *it is greatly intensified by the resistance* [ital. added], . . . ; and thirdly, it is lacking . . . in a regard for reality, is less sensible, less concerned about consequences and more blind in its valuation of the loved person . . . [pp. 168–169]. . . . Again, when a woman sues for love, to reject and refuse is a distressing part for a man to play; and, in spite of neurosis and resistance, there is an incomparable fascination in a woman of high principles who confesses her passion [p. 170].

This potentially interactive development is primarily an instance of structural actuality of the transference. Its effects may be elaborated into a transference–countertransference enactment.

Intimate strivings in general are linked with agon, which in fact contains aggression in its myriad forms no less than love. These real qualities of the affective ambiance are not necessarily metaphorically elaborated by the analyst as would be the case with a countertransference response. With anticipation of agon and awareness of these structural features, the induced affect becomes an aim-inhibited signal and the agon is restrained and limited.

Transference in general profoundly influences and may be influenced by a number of intrapsychic and interactional tensions, along the axes of intimacy/distance, dominance/submission, independence/dependence, love/hate, etc. Not all responses to these influences are countertransference. For instance, a patient rejects the use of the couch, and in further defensiveness she employs the face-to-face sessions to evaluate the analyst's facial and postural changes as indices of his reliability, commitment, and sincerity. For the analyst, this was a moderately discomforting resistance threatening his work. However, her struggle for control did not entangle him. Instead, he persevered in a limited struggle to analyze and understand her resistance. Over time, the patient reduced her control through the insight that she had been made anxious by her conflicted sense of dependence and isolation during her previous analysis, an anxiety that in turn had its history in her experiences with her depressive, recurrently abdicating mother and her guilty closeness to her seductive father.

Separation and loss, control of anxiety through control of others, and conflicts of intimacy and dependence were prominent in the dynamics of her transference enactments, and prominent structures of her transference, both extra-analytically and during sessions. Since adolescence, these had led either into unwittingly seductive entanglements or into often unrealistic avoidant behavior. Transference wishes and anxieties were externalized into conflicted struggles with the analyst. It is my impression that in her previous analysis, the analyst had defensively counterresisted, forestalling the patient's full expression and working through of her own agonistic maneuvers. Changing meanings of her behavior were variously expressed over a period of time, rendering the second analyst's perceptions inexact and delayed. This was not owing to his being seduced or induced into an agon as distinguished from his struggle with her resistance toward meaning in a psychoanalytic context.

Freud recognized the agon or struggle of transference. I mention this to suggest that transference as agon has long been known tacitly though seldom named as such. In 1914 (p. 154; ital. added) he wrote of admitting: "the compulsion to repeat . . . into the *transference as a playground* in which it is allowed to expand in almost complete freedom and . . . display to us everything . . . that is hidden in the patient's mind. . . giving all the symptoms of the illness *a new transference meaning* and . . . replacing his ordinary neurosis by a 'transference neurosis' of which he can be cured. . . ."

"Playground," in the first italicized phrase, is better translated from the German *Tummelplatz* as "rumpus place," "romp place," or even as "rough-house" (or so I am informed). Earlier in the same paper Freud had referred to a "perpetual *struggle* . . . to keep in the psychical sphere all the impulses which the patient would like to direct into the motor sphere" (p. 153; ital. added).

Multiple, Changing Meanings; Transference as Deception

> It must not be forgotten that the things one hears are for the most part things whose meaning is only recognized later on.
>
> —Freud, 1912, p. 112

The epigraph points to frequent and inherent sources of delay in the analyst's comprehension and responsiveness. It is not only the distractions of agons that cause transference and its meanings to be overlooked or tardily perceived. People are bundles of contradictions at all levels of functioning. In any patient, transference is protean, its meanings changing as the patterns of conflict and defense change. As an analysis progresses, the diagnostic category may change. The fullest comprehension of the transference in a complete configuration may be accomplished only in the final phases of the work.

Owing to continuing shifts of conflict and defense, including the faltering of motivation when resistances are mobilized, patients who otherwise commit time, money, and energy to their analyses may nevertheless resort to what in any other context would surely be regarded as deception and duplicity. Abuse of free association is often more prominent than its use, and is often close to a deliberate, conscious decision and control. Resistances may be rationalized brazenly with no way for the analyst to test their veracity.

In these ways patients are often plausible but neither authentic nor sincere. Without pejorative intent, this phrasing could be included in a definition of transference. I think it was Hartmann who defined psychoanalysis as the study of self-deception and its motives. I venture to add: "including the *projected or externalized* deceptions, with their effects on the analyst, that the analysand must resort to in order to sustain the self-deceptions."

The resultant clouding of meaning is a continuing source of tension for the analyst, whose adaptiveness is thereby placed on trial. Although by training and aptitude analysts are tolerant of doubt and ambiguity, of the passage of time, of pain and other affects, repeated frustration can undermine healthy narcissistic investments in the work and carries its own adverse consequences.

To repeat, agonistic confusion and/or delayed perception of the fact and meaning of a transference are real effects of actual qualities of the transference. Other possible sources of these phenomena lie in countertransference and, *horribile dictu,* even in the analyst's ineptness or ignorance. Leaving aside these awkwardnesses, it is conducive to clear observation and thinking to consider actualities of transference structure, thereby anticipating and preventing agonistic confusions or delayed perceptions.

Countertransference is an ambiguous explanation for mismanagements and successes. It denotes only the psychology of the analyst, largely omitting the important details of interaction between two persons. We have tended to overlook the potency of the shifting meanings, affective ambiances, and induced agons, viewed as part of transference structure, that initiate and induce many of the analyst's misperceptions and other errors of stance and technique, short of countertransference. Effects of transference structure reflect the inherent internal shifts in conflicts and defenses and are prone to occur aside from effects of the analyst as an actual or transference presence.

Vignette: Perceptions of Shifting Transference Meanings and Agons

A patient announces, after a month of controlling the sessions by repetitious recounting of her successful living, that she has been increasingly annoyed with the analyst. She wants him to tell her what a "good woman" she is. She demands tangible and frequent assertions to this effect, as though to confirm her buoyant self-esteem.

Taken aback and puzzled by this barrage of angry reproaches and having already, during her account of successful and happy living, oscillated between skepticism and boredom, never convinced that this was other than a transparent flight into health under the auspices of a positive transference, the analyst thought he now discerned a pattern—that she was demanding from him what she had obtained from her previous therapist (and lover), with whom she had enacted mother- and father-transference fantasies. This formulation produced a flat negative—not surprisingly, for it had been a "reflex" effort by him to ward off the anxiety of her baffling reproaches.

The previous analysis had foundered into a prolonged, mutually seductive and financial exploitation, each by the dependently controlling other. During her childhood, her father had been, if not sexually seducing, certainly seductive in his preference for her as a little girl over his increasingly disturbed wife.

The patient was a flirtatious woman who denied awareness of this. There had been every expectation that a manifest erotized transference would again develop. It did not until much later, after the events reported here, though several times she had spontaneously been at pains to assert its absence. She had already spoken of her need to control others, mostly in the context of her wish for "empowerment," a buzzword she often used to indicate her fantasied antidote to the helpless anxiety of abandonment. This she had experienced throughout her life, exacerbated yet again with the termination of the lengthy, mutually deceptive period of transference acting out in her previous treatment. Discharged from that relationship, she had spent the first 18 months in the new analysis in a miserably depressed state, painfully depleted in self-esteem, helplessly angry, and agitated, duplicating earlier reasons for initially entering treatment.

There were no noteworthy changes during the next several weeks. The analyst remained uninvolved in any specific, mutual agon, but continued to work within the puzzling framework of shifting and uncertain meanings. That is, he awaited further developments in her enactment; his clinical judgment, based upon his working model of the patient, cautioned that he not intervene now. This constituted a limited agon with the patient, who was angrily frustrated and frustrating, her attitude partly translatable as, "If he won't love me as I wish, as least I'll get him to fight with me." Unwilling as the analyst was to be included in these enactments, the agon was unavoidable; inasmuch as it was limited, it eventually opened to clarification and interpretation.

Definitive clarification came after the patient made a surprise visit to her former therapist. She had been talking about wanting to make such a visit and had tolerated no attempted clarifications from the analyst nor interference from a close confidante (of whom more later). They talked and embraced briefly, and she left in high spirits. Still elated, she described the experience to her current analyst in some detail. Sensing strongly that her conduct veiled still further meaning, he could only inquire for more associational details. She had since awaited a phone call from the former lover, but it did not come to pass. She also told her intimate woman friend and confidante of her visit. The friend, who had been expressing alarmed reproof at her exposing herself to further anguish, asked whether she had felt an "oedipal triumph" over the therapist's wife. Reporting this exchange to the present analyst, the patient now reproached him with not having raised this question with her. Setting confidante and analyst against each other, she was at last exposing the key to her cryptic messages, giving information that explained her behavior. Now, the analyst interpreted that any intended triumph was surely of the two women over each of the two men. She became thoughtfully silent, and he went on to review the several overlapping triangular relationships that were involved, all repeating, like variations on a theme, her behavior as a little girl. She had shuttled between her parents, her mother criticizing the father and accusing her of disloyalty, and her father admonishing the child not to be like her mother, while she anxiously worked at controlling her sources of narcissistic supply. The patient's behavior recapitulated whole segments of her childhood—the repeated periods of unhappy solitude, awaiting her father's visits; her struggles against the angry reproaches of her mother; and her repeated disappointments when father departed without her. Her reproaches of the analyst were displacements from her parents, her husband, and her former lover.

It is not uncommon for an analyst to have access to all of the pertinent facts fueling a transference enactment, but to be handicapped from organizing them into a timely and accurate interpretation until the patient gives some indication that he or she is ready to participate in a systematization of those facts. The analyst will have awaited his opportune moment to intervene, a moment that comes, as in this vignette, with the patient's beginning restructuring of the resistance. The analyst had been assisted here in sensing the direction the patient was taking through his not having been caught up in the agon she was projecting and externalizing. Until she had enacted her own struggle, the shifting meanings of the transference remained obscure. In effect, the analyst relied successfully on appropriate concern for the patient, collecting data selectively, and not seeking actively after meaning, but awaiting signs of the patient's readiness to avow the transference resistance and its meanings.

Repetitive Themes in Transference

Repetitive themes may be structured in the transference for a variety of reasons: e.g., belated mastery of unassimilated anxiety; repeated striving toward a gratification that instead evokes painful affect; a process of undoing that is intended, but fails, to reach expiation through sequences of repetition. A common denominator of these dynamics is the attaining of the operation of a constancy principle that is comparable to the physiological concept of homeostasis (see Laplanche & Pontalis, 1973, pp. 343, 346).

The well-known repetitiveness of transference themes constitutes a part of transference structuring and contributes further to the effects on the analyst of affective ambiance, changing meanings, and the threat of agons. As with the two vignettes described, even with changing meanings one can discern a central core of repetition. Common meanings gradually emerge.

A regressive pull is central to the repetition. The analyst may experience the regression and the repetition as a demanding insistence upon intervention; a consequent agonistic involvement may progress to a countertransference response. The patient's repeated efforts to integrate that which was lost, lacking, or otherwise distorted may be temporarily overlooked. These patterns and their shifting meanings can have a stultifying effect on the analyst, inducing states co-responsive to the patient's underlying despair and anger—a not uncommon development, for instance, in the presence of the negative therapeutic reaction.

Meaning and the Reversal of Agonistic Puzzlement: Loss and Empathy

Dealing with the multiple, changing meanings of the transference and of transference as deception I earlier indicated that the effects of these structural actualities of the transference were to leave the analyst in a state of perplexity and puzzlement.

The presence of these perplexed states should, in the first place, inform the analyst that he is probably experiencing the effects of an active transference. The loss of meaning through the patient's deceptive maneuvers will ordinarily activate the analyst to take steps to rectify his state of mystification, if only to review and to listen more carefully for the meaning of the stoppage. As to this, I may say that the cognitive-affective meaning sought in psychoanalysis is an index of, as well as a linkage with, what Loewald (1979) referred to as the "mutual engagement" that is directly involved in understanding the patient. Whether arrived at through association or by means of configurational, holistic patterns (exemplified in Freud's [1896, p. 192] comments about *"Saxa loquuntur!"* [Let the stones talk] or in the history of Kékulé's creative invention of the benzene ring in organic chemistry), "meaning" is a process of connections and contexts transacted between systems, both within a person and between persons. A patient's progressive recognition that her/his actions, feelings, and thoughts have meaning assists him in the discovery that he can be understood in a continuing psychoanalytic interaction with another person, offering him access to a new sense of self and eventually to a hitherto absent freedom of choice in his way of living. "Meaning" thereby is a profoundly important cognitive-affective phenomenon, one that carries much of the weight of the treatment processes. Loewald's observation is of a situation of affective relevancy of analyst and analysand to each other, of a working rapport or alliance, and of trial identifications. The disruption of this form of relevancy by the patient's resistance is often accomplished so indirectly and unexpectedly as to result in the analyst's mystification and failure of clinical judgment and acumen. The work is now obscured and the relationship unbalanced. It is observable that the analyst's puzzlement is accompanied with a vague or rudimentary sense of yearning or longing toward a return of the prior mutuality, however limited it may have been, or even if it had consisted merely of an expectation of mutual engagement. The analyst, and perhaps also the patient, may experience a sense of frustration in the form of boredom, sleepiness, irritation, or other response. Beyond this, a pertinent sense of sadness is frequently evident, highlighting the fact of loss.

The central fact here is that there is an effort at problem-solving fed by the motivation that has drawn the analyst into his vocation. There is a "leaning" toward understanding the problems represented in and by the other person.

David Rapaport wrote of the analyst's need for "nutriment" derived from the patient's adequate verbalizations, in order to facilitate the analyst's developing of the analytic process (1967). I would add, bearing further on the orality of these matters, that a sense of loss, distance, and yearning for reengagement, i.e., a degree of grieving or of the affect of sadness, have long been recognized as the precursors and stimuli of empathic insight (Greenson, 1960; Olinick, 1969). To have lost mutual engagement with the patient becomes a potent excitant for seeking meaning through empathic perception and integration, and thereby toward reestablishing rapport and a sense of order. Clinical judgment and inference can then operate once again.

Because of the anaclitic origins and nature of this dependent "leaning" toward renewal and reestablishing of a relationship, there may ensue an untoward sympathy, an overidentification with the analysand. Alertness to this possibility leads to utilizing that tendency as an affect-signal, halting unwarranted developments. In any case, empathy—the trial identification alluded to earlier—must be distinguished from sympathy, the latter being more likely to issue in compassionately motivated, but inappropriate action (Olinick, 1984). Empathy is a primitive, delicate instrument, but it is honed to great skill and precision by a number of clinicians. As a "feeling into" it generates meaning. In this sense, empathy and its evoking of meaning provide a cognitive-affective linkage with a lost object, i.e., with the patient whose transference structure effects a defensive distancing and obfuscating of the work.

As intersystemic processes uniting apparently disparate matters into decoded unitary meanings, the phenomena of meaning and of empathic integration have further connections. Empathy unites the analyst's discrete perceptions, his working model of the patient, and his own imaginative judgment into meaningful configurations. There is formed a synesthetic, metaphorized aggregation of perceptions—a potential configuration of meanings—bearing upon the patient (Olinick, 1976). Its intersystemic quality, from person to person and among a variety of internal functions, moves from puzzlement and a sense of loss to a reorganizing of the field into new meanings that may now be processed into appropriate interventions. This development constitutes an effective method of working through the barriers to understanding that are set up by the built-in, behavioral, communicational structures of the patient's transference.

Conclusions

The distinctions I have outlined between the analyst's responses to the structural features of the transference and the analyst's countertransference responses are not always clearly defined "either-or" categories. But classification difficulties and quandaries do not mean there are no distinctions, only that there are shadings. The issues have understandably long been by-passed and neglected. During an earlier period of psychoanalysis, any problems experienced by the analyst tended to have been attributed to countertransference, often with the innuendo that his or her training analysis was incomplete. In the 1950s, the problem was fitted to a solution through the proposition that countertransference was a boon: like transference, it was not solely an obstacle to treatment but, rather, through it one could "read" the patient. Still, problems continued with the transference per se, for transference, as we have come to recognize, has not only an intrapsychic function, but is interactional as well. Both sets of functions work toward alloplastic compensations and compromises in the service of conflictual defenses. One must conclude that what I have designated here "actual reactions to the structure of transference" are never far from countertransference reactions.

REFERENCES

Bird, B. (1972). Notes on transference: Universal phenomenon and hardest part of analysis. *J. Amer. Psychoanal. Assn.*, 20:267–301.

Boesky, D. (1990). The psychoanalytic process and its components. *Psychoanal. Quart.*, 50:550–584.

Freud, S. (1896). The aetiology of hysteria. *S.E.*, 3.

_____ (1912). Recommendations to physicians practicing psycho-analysis. *S.E.*, 12.
_____ (1914). Remembering, repeating, and working through. *S.E.*, 12.
Greenson, R. (1960). Empathy and its vicissitudes. *Internat. J. Psycho-Anal.*, 41:418–424.
Laplanche, J. & Pontalis, J. B. (1973). *The Language of Psycho-Analysis*. New York: Norton.
Loewald, H. (1979). Reflections on the psychoanalytic process and its therapeutic potential. *The Psychoanalytic Study of the Child*, 34:155–168. New Haven, CT: Yale Univ. Press.
Olinick, S. (1969). Empathy and regression. In *The Psychotherapeutic Instrument*. New York: Aronson, 1980, pp. 3–16.
_____ (1976). Empathy and metaphoric correspondences. *Ann. Psychoanal.*, 4:93–100.
_____ (1984). A critique of empathy and sympathy. In *Empathy I*, ed. J. Lichtenberg, M. Bornstein & D. Silver. Hillsdale, NJ: The Analytic Press, pp. 137–166.
_____ (1989). Changing psychic structures through treatment: Criteria for change. *J. Amer. Psychoanal. Assn.*, 37:639–654.
_____ (1992). Nostalgia and transference. *Contemp. Psychoanal.*, 28:195–198.
Rapaport, D. (1967). *The Collected Papers of David Rapaport*, ed. M. M. Gill. New York: Basic Books.
Sandler, J. (1976). Countertransference and role responsiveness. *Internat. Rev. Psycho-Anal.*, 3:32–37.

2819 Ellicott Street, NW
Washington, DC 20008

Unconscious Fantasy and Theories of Technique

FREDERIC J. LEVINE, Ph.D.

> All analysts recognize the need for deprivations in psychoanalysis; they would also agree in principle on the analyst's need to be human. The problem arises, however, in determining what is meant by humanness in the analytic situation and how does one reconcile it with the principle of deprivation [Greenson, 1965].

THERE HAVE ALWAYS BEEN DIFFERENCES OF OPINION among analysts about the day-to-day management of what most consider the "gold" of transference analysis and the "baser metals" of other psychoanalytic procedures; but only since the 1950s has an extensive literature developed about the technical handling of various components of the analytic relationship (Shapiro, 1961; Greenson, 1965); and that literature is filled with controversy. I am referring here to discussions of two groups of concepts: On the one hand are "the real relationship," "therapeutic alliance," "working alliance," and "empathic responsiveness," all of which denote interpersonal processes, which some view as having a major influence on the course or outcome of analysis. On the other hand is a set of concepts that Freud originally introduced, which is sometimes counterpoised to the first group as providing

Dr. Levine is a member of the faculty at the Institute of the Philadelphia Association for Psychoanalysis; he is a Training and Supervising Analyst at the New York Freudian Society.

more classical guidelines for the "appropriate" manifest behavior of the analyst: These include "the rule of abstinence," "blank screen," "neutrality," and the like. Both sets of concepts often appear in discussions of the technical problems of how to differentiate and manage transference and nontransference aspects of the analytic relationship; it is in regard to this central concern that they have been controversial. In what follows, after reviewing the major features of this controversy, I offer a hypothesis about its causes which I believe sheds light on some of the most vexing problems of psychoanalytic theorizing, and on an important root of the pervasive tendency for analysts to become fractionated into competing schools of thought.

I do not "take sides" in the controversy, nor propose a new solution to it. Instead, I suggest that the often vehement disputes about manifest features of analytic technique have arisen partly because theories about the analytic relationship tend to be colored and shaped by a particular set of unconscious connotative meanings (that is, by certain transferences) which are readily and commonly projected onto the analyst and the analytic process by patients and by at least some analysts and analytic theorists as well.[1] A hallmark of this process, which I believe is evidence that it actually does occur, is that we can often observe that the definitions and uses of certain of our technical terms change over the course of time, in predictable ways that reflect the influence of these projections. I hope to illustrate how this phenomenon has affected the semantic natural histories of a few of our technical terms.

Review of the Controversy

In their 1969 paper on the "non-transference" relationship in analysis, Greenson and Wexler said it was a "sensitive" matter to theorize about nontransference factors. They quoted Anna

[1]As Abend (1979), Arlow (1981), and Reed (1984) have shown, psychoanalytic technical terms and theories are, like all else that is human, compromise formations, "based in part on shared unconscious fantasy and in part on communality of clinical experience and training" (Reed, 1984, p. 10).

Freud's statement that the notion of a "real" relationship between patient and analyst was valuable but "technically subversive," and said that it was a topic previous authors had evaded (1969). Their use of this strong language is one among many bits of evidence that could be cited to show that the subject of how to understand and manage the analytic relationship has never been merely a scientific question, but is fraught with an emotional significance that has sometimes led to schisms and *ad hominem* disagreements among analysts.

The substance of the controversy can be roughly characterized by two schematically presented positions: One group of analysts values and stresses the role of "real" factors in the analytic relationship, particularly the patient's perception of the analyst's actual idiosyncracies, character, empathy, and the like; while a second approach cautions against laying stress on distinctions between analyzable transference and other relationship "factors," except as matters of tact. Analysts who favor recognizing or emphasizing "real" or nontransference factors, do so for a number of reasons. Some merely distinguish what Freud (1912, p. 105) called "unobjectionable" parts of the relationship from analyzable transference, and leave these uninterpreted in order to enhance the patient-analyst collaboration. For others, these perceptions and impressions of the analyst are not parts of the transference at all but must be respected as expressions of the patient's realistic ego functioning (Greenson & Wexler, 1969). And a third group not only sees the patient's overt experience of the analyst as outside transference but considers it a major curative force in its own right. A number of analysts who place weight on "real" relationship components have pointed out that the more classical approach is sometimes pursued in an extreme fashion which "creates an analytic climate not of neutrality . . . but of deprivation" (Viederman, 1991, p. 453).

On the other hand, analysts who deemphasize distinctions between the analysand's transference and "real" experiences tend to conceptualize interpretation leading to insight as the main curative factor in psychoanalysis proper (Gray's [1991] "essential psychoanalysis") and to be alert to the "danger" of actions by the analyst that might exclude one or another aspect of the relationship from analytic scrutiny and thus restrict a patient's capacity to gain insight into his/her transference. These analysts often suggest that those who emphasize nontransference factors run the risk of enacting transference demands rather than analyzing them, and of tending toward "wild" analysis, corrective emotional experience, or cure through love. These broad antithetical positions are the essence of the controversy.

I believe that over and above the rational, scientific bases of this controversy, it has important roots in a particular unconscious tendency (on the part of patients and theorists alike) to imbue the analytic task and the analyst's person and behavior with punitive, idealized, or soothing and permissive characteristics, and that these attributions are derived from externalizations of infantile representations of the parents (i.e., the superego). These externalizations, which are created primarily for defensive purposes, color the analysis and result in the analyst's being selectively perceived or misperceived—at times as warm, supportive and gratifying (or seductive), at others as impressive and ideal, and at still others as disapproving or frustrating toward the patient's wishes and strivings. Although these distortions occur for intrapsychic reasons, analysts sometimes try to compensate for them by acting in an opposite way (which is also parental in nature), and they may then build these enactments into theories. I therefore suggest that the controversy under scrutiny might be clarified if it is studied *as a unit:* if the two antithetical, competing approaches to the analytic relationship are seen as opposite ends of a continuum—opposing manifestations of a single underlying conflictual fantasy-system. The tension created by this conflict leaves its traces in a particular trend in theories and technical recommendations which I am calling "conceptual drift."

In brief, by "conceptual drift" I mean that concepts (such as therapeutic alliance, on the one hand, and "abstinence," on the other) which were originally introduced as guides to help the analyst sort out conflictual and other meanings of the relationship (that is, to help him/her be more effective in observing and understanding transference) often undergo a characteristic metamorphosis over the course of time—a change of meaning and/or usage, through which they gradually come to express the very conflicts which they were introduced to manage. Their original very specific technical meanings become broadened, and they are liable to be concretized into entities or "parts" of the relationship, and to take on a "reality" justified not by the original definitions but by shared unconscious forces. This may contaminate the way the analyst perceives the goals and methods of treatment and drive him/her away from neutrality. Characteristically, conceptual drift causes concepts whose principal original meanings referred to the analyst's observing and data-gathering activities to be subtly redefined so that they become forms of action that the analyst may take toward the patient: interventions, or methods of molding the relationship, or ways of providing models or "nutriment." Borrowing terms from neurology and general psychology, it may be helpful to think of conceptual drift as entailing a change in the referents of these concepts *from* the analyst's afferent or receptive processes *to* his/her efferent or expressive functions toward the analysand. This is often part of a broad shift in how the locus of curative power in the analytic relationship is conceptualized, toward having it reside largely in the analyst, whose role is seen as having explicit or implied parentlike qualities.

Connotations of the Analytic Process

It has long been recognized that the analyst and the psychoanalytic process are commonly interpreted by patients in ways derived from the superego's infantile images of parental censure and approval (Strachey, 1934). A starting point for understanding how and why these particular meanings occur so universally can be found in Lewin's (1954, 1955) classic formulation that the interplay of reality and fantasy in patients' mental processes during analysis has important connections with states of sleep, dreaming, and wakefulness. Lewin described the essential balance and oscillation during analysis between states of consciousness approaching sleep and others which approach wakefulness. Further, he called attention to the tendency of psychoanalytic treatment, which is the heir of hypnosis, anaesthesia, and other historical "sleep treatments," to evoke characteristic wishes and fears regarding uncontrolled expression of erotic and hostile primitive impulses—fears that have been the age-old accompaniments of these treatments: for example, seduction by a Svengali. These common wishes and fears were reflected in the associations of a young woman who dreamed of herself, at the start of analysis, as Nabokov's Lolita, with the analyst as Lolita's elderly seducer, Humbert Humbert. It subsequently emerged that in the past the patient had been molested by older men whom she had depended on as experts and guides, like the analyst, and she feared another betrayal. But being vulnerable also had an appeal: she imagined that it would be easiest to lose her virginity while she was asleep, when she could neither resist a seduction nor feel responsible for its results. These fantasies were reevoked by her unconscious linkage of the analytic situation with sleep and dreaming.

Lewin pointed out that fantasies of this type influence the way the analyst's interpretations are perceived. When looked at as "background music," as an action by one person toward another, rather than in terms of the particular contents being communicated, interpretation appears Janus-faced: When analyzing resistances to free association, the analyst encourages the analysand to regress (i.e., to "sleep")—and in so doing is seen as seductive and/or soothing; and then periodically the analyst "awakens" the analysand by making interpretations. The analyst's need to periodically disturb the patient's "sleep"-like associative process makes it inevitable that patients will often associate the analyst's interpretations with punitive features of their superegos—the censorious sleep-disturber of the mind.

If we now consider these issues from the added vantage point of Gray's (1987, 1991) recent formulation that the superego is essentially a system of defenses *within the ego* and constitutes a major part of the analyzable transference, we can apply Lewin's (1954) ideas more broadly, to the entire analytic situation and the analyst's role. According to Gray, when any relationship threatens to arouse conflictual impulses (as analysis does) there is a tendency to externalize prohibitions and harsh representations—or comforting ones—drawn from the individual's store of infantile parental introjects, onto the object (that is, the analyst) and onto the parameters of the relationship, for defensive purposes. The analyst becomes converted into a replica of infantile images of the judgmental, punitive, or forgiving parents in order to ward off the anxiety aroused by the potential impulse expression. (We are all familiar with patients who hear the analyst's every breath or movement in the chair as a sign of criticism and disparagement, and with others who bask blissfully in the sound of the analyst's warm and soothing voice.) It is this duality in the functions and representations projected onto the analysis and the analyst for defensive purposes which, I suggest, accounts for the polarization of theories about the analytic relationship.

In keeping with contemporary formulations (Abend, 1979; Arlow, 1981), I assume that transference fantasies of these kinds are not limited to patients, but often play an important role in the analyst's functioning and in theory-building as well (depending on their correspondence with the analyst's or theoretician's own repressed conflicts). I am not implying that these theories are necessarily flawed: "the correctness of a given scientific theory . . . has only to do with its consonance with the data it seeks to explain, not at all with its relation to the unconscious mind of its author" (Abend, 1979, pp. 589–590). In the present instance, however, I believe that the strength of the controversies about managing the analytic relationship does reflect regressive influences. Let me now offer evidence of how concepts about the analytic relationship become problematic because they are superimposed on these underlying fantasies.

The "Real" Relationship

I know that a newspaper account is not a scientific document, but one such that caught my eye several years ago depicts the issue at hand with a directness not usually found in technical literature, tempting me to use it as a springboard for the more customary type of evidence that follows it.

The article appeared in the *New York Times,* September 26, 1986, in conjunction with the release of a film, "That's Life," by Blake Edwards. What was noteworthy was that the film was co-authored by Mr. Edwards and his psychoanalyst, Milton Wexler. When interviewed about his decision to collaborate with a patient (which I certainly am not questioning, since I know nothing about the particular case), Wexler was quoted as speaking in a tone of playful sarcasm that I think illustrates analysts' polarization:

"Every strict Freudian will think this collaboration is anathema. I was a classical analyst 100 years ago in New York, but now I'm too old to be so stuffy." He went on to say that, although he recognized the close contact with a patient could be seen as interfering with transference, "I don't think transference is so important anymore. . . . I think that . . . the real opportunity to identify with the therapist and have a real relationship with him are more important."

Wexler appears to have here used the word *real,* in the "real relationship," in a particular way: to refer to manifest behavior which is treated as *other than transference.* This is a very different usage from what he and Greenson had in mind when they originally introduced the concept, but one that I believe has come to be common in our literature. It is similar to certain meanings which may be implied when the word *real* is emphasized in the course of a patient's associations, and which may signal a defensively based wish to treat a subject at a manifest level only, and exclude it from analysis. Real can mean *free of intrapsychic conflict,* as in "my headache has real physiological causes, it's not 'all in my head,' " or "in addition to emotional problems I have difficulties in the real world." It can also mean *caused by external matters outside the individual's control,* for which he/she is *therefore not blameworthy* (like the woman who wanted to lose her virginity in her sleep)—i.e., not to be punished by the individual's infantile parental introjects as represented externally in the person of the analyst. These uses of *real* may have the additional goal of denigrating the analysis and the importance of the unconscious, to reinforce the defense.

Back in 1969 when Wexler collaborated with Greenson on one of the highly influential papers that introduced the concept of "real relationship," the principal definition of that term was much narrower, as a companion to, and enhancer of, the analysis of transference. "We want to state our basic propositions: to facilitate the full flowering and ultimate resolution of the patient's transference reactions, it is essential in all cases to recognize, acknowledge, clarify, differentiate and even nurture the nontransference or relatively transference-free reactions between patient and analyst" (Greenson & Wexler, 1969, p. 361). That paper adumbrated the following views on the technical linkages between the "real" relationship and transference analysis: All object relationships contain mixtures of realistic and transferential elements. Many psychoanalysts apply Freud's concepts of the analyst as mirror and the rule of abstinence in exaggerated ways which "may stifle the development and clarification of the transference neurosis" (p. 361). To remedy this rigidity, a clear-cut distinction should be drawn between transference and relatively transference-free aspects of the relationship, because the nontransference, "real" relationship forms the core of a "rapport which . . . enables the patient to work purposefully in the analytic situation despite his transference . . . [and] to endure the long and often painful process of working through." They emphasized that they did "not deny the central importance of transference interpretations in psychoanalysis," but they also felt that patients "need the experience of having their appropriate ego functions and object relationships acknowledged and respected" (pp. 373-385). If the *New York Times* article is an accurate reflection of Wexler's later views, there was not only a radical revision of his thinking about transference, but also a marked conceptual drift in the way he used the concept of "real relationship." It was no longer merely a technical factor that facilitates effective analysis but had become the central mechanism of cure, replacing transference analysis itself.

More significant is that Wexler was not alone. A survey of recent literature on the "real relationship" reveals a number of instances of similar drift: The "real relationship" may move from being largely unplanned and incidental to being actively manipulated by the analyst; from being defined primarily in terms of the analyst's perceptions and observations about the patient to requiring activity on the part of the analyst (from afferent to efferent); from being mainly an aid in analyzing transference and avoiding iatrogenic difficulties to—sometimes—being seen as having a directly beneficial effect on the patient (another efferent characteristic). In all these forms the shift is toward viewing the analyst as increasingly active and influential with respect to a relatively more passive patient—which is the kind of change that would be an expected concomitant of projecting infantile images of the parents onto the analyst.

For example, Dewald is one of a number of analysts who

conceptualize the "real" patient-analyst relationship as neither entirely one of transference nor a purely contemporary experience, but as having features of both: The image of the analyst constitutes "a real and new experience at the patient's neurotic level of . . . adaptation [which] serves as a new model of interpersonal interaction" (Dewald, 1976, pp. 217–218). For those who take this point of view, the analyst's neutral, dependable behavior and nonreactive tolerance of the patient's associations are no longer merely vantage points for observation, they acquire efferent, influential *properties* which "provide the patient with the experience of 'a good parent' who encourages his child to face new and frightening danger situations, [and] . . . *can* know what is in his mind and . . . still accept him [even when he had been via the transference] anticipating a critical, judgmental . . . praising, rejecting . . . or seductive response" (pp. 218–220). This formulation shows how the analyst's behavior, which originally had only receptive purposes, drifts into being conceptualized as a form of action by acquiring parental connotations which have unrecognized defensive and potentially analyzable meanings. It redefines analytic neutrality as a kind of silent action: enacting a contradiction to the patient's transference expectations, instead of analyzing them.

A somewhat greater drift occurs in the views of analysts who see the "real" relationship as a nexus for internalization and identification processes from which a patient can "internalize qualities . . . of the analyst that are missing in himself" (Adler, 1980, p. 554), and "perceive the objective personal qualities of their analyst and utilize them for internalizations" (p. 555). When the relationship is viewed as being an important directly curative force in these ways, it may no longer seem sufficient merely to allow it to develop as a by-product of the analyst's uncontrived demeanor. Instead, analysts may be urged to present themselves in special ways intended to help establish and strengthen this potentially curative bond—e.g., to make "judicious" use of "alliance-building statements" emphasizing the word "we" (Adler, p. 555). Again, this is a move toward greater activity and parent-like influence for the analyst.

In addition, from the perspective of analysts who believe that patients do not simply form identifications with an "objective" analyst, but with an image of the analyst that is partly composed of transferences, identifications "may [even] solidify the neurosis by crystallizing and fixing some aspect of the transference" (Arlow, 1981, p. 491); and these methods would change the real relationship from being a facilitator of defense analysis to a possible source of defense building.

Conceptual Drift: The Example of "Empathy"

A relative newcomer to the psychoanalytic lexicon, "empathy" was first conceptualized by Kohut within a classical psychoanalytic framework; he then made it a cornerstone of his self psychology. As he did so, his use of the term underwent a gradual conceptual drift.

Kohut (1959) originally described empathy as the analyst's central *mental process,* defined as "vicarious introspection"—imagining oneself in another's situation and then looking within oneself, in this imagined position, to experience how the other person thinks or feels. Kohut saw empathy as defining the analytic method of observation: "We speak of physical phenomena when the essential ingredient of our observational methods includes our senses, we speak of psychological phenomena when the essential ingredient . . . is introspection and empathy" used to infer the purpose or personal meaning of another person's actions (p. 460). At that stage of his thinking Kohut defined empathy exclusively as involving receptive functions of the analyst, but as Self Psychology developed, the term acquired decidedly more efferent or communicative meanings: First, through a developmental stress on the traumatic effects of what were called parental "failures" of empathy—i.e., children's perceptions of unempathic responses from their parents—empathy was silently redefined as a force that had impact on others. It subsequently evolved further into a form of interpersonal communication and influence.

In Kohut's last book, *How Does Analysis Cure?* (1984), empathy retains its original receptive meaning, but by now is also seen as a fundamental component of the analyst's interpretive activity: In making an interpretation, "the analyst verbalizes . . . that he has grasped what the patient feels; . . . thus demonstrating to him that he has been 'understood,' that is, that another person has been able to experience . . . what he himself has experienced" (pp. 176–177). And much of the mutative effect of an interpretation "is also based on empathy. . . . In a certain sense . . . correct dynamic interpretations and genetic reconstructions provide no more for the analysand than further proof that another person has understood him" (p. 184).

Kohut's use of the word "understand" here exemplifies the subtle shift in the meaning of empathy from its original receptive role as a tool of the secondary process, with which the analyst *understands*—i.e., *gains knowledge of* the patient, to becoming an expression of primitive parentally derived functions. As a communication of forgiveness and reassurance through "understanding," the primary message of an interpretation does not lie in its verbalized content, but in the fact that it demonstrates the analyst's empathic "understanding," i.e., acceptance. In this formulation, what is usually the background music (Lewin, 1954, p. 507) of psychoanalysis has become its central feature, and what had been in the foreground is moved to the periphery, and even that, perhaps, only nominally.

Conceptual Drift—The "Analytic Vacuum," and the Authoritarian Analyst

Both Kohut and Greenson introduced their modifications of theory and technique to correct what they saw as counterproductive trends in psychoanalytic practice. Kohut (1984) found that classical analysts often were moralistic and rule-bound, opposing patients' wishes for gratification (p. 82), overzealously trying to "do away with" (p. 147) resistances, and portraying themselves as unnaturally unemotional. These criticisms were not unique or idiosyncratic: so many observers have echoed Kohut's charge that "the actual practice of analysis is burdened by . . . hidden moral and educational goals" (1984, p. 208) as to make it apparent that it has some validity. Stone, for example, after describing what he called the "intrinsic formal stringencies" of the analytic situation (e.g., the analyst remaining outside the patient's line of sight, the stereotyped schedule, the limitation of responses mostly to interpretation) as creating a beneficial "analytic vacuum," warned against exaggerating these deprivations: "may not the trend toward a schematic perfection in carrying out the principle of abstinence . . . have . . . subtly . . . produced technical difficulties of paradoxical character?" (1961, pp. 107–108), he asks.

The immediate relevance of these observations is that this kind of behavior—with its emphasis on manifest forms and procedures rather than on their personal meanings to particular patients—is another example of conceptual drift, this time regarding the meaning and use of Freud's few suggestions about the analyst's behavior and attitude. Lipton (1977) believed that although Freud's own technique was both human and humane, after Freud's death a "significant change in technique came into being, largely unrecognized." According to Lipton, this "redefinition of the concept of technique . . . tends to foster artificiality; tends to give undue weight to the analyst's [manifest] behaviour; tends to expand technique beyond the area which the patient knows about and collaborates with; and tends to substitute for the genuine, personal relationship on which the analysis is based an idealized relationship in which the patient meets not another person but a sort of encompassing, technically-correct instrumentality" (p. 266). As he demonstrated, the basis for this redefinition was an unremarked concretization of Freud's technical principles, which "tends to move from the position in which the analyst's technique is judged according to his purpose to one in which [it] is judged according to his behaviour" (p. 262). In light of the present considerations we can see that the shape taken by these changes had typical features of conceptual drift: a focus on concrete, manifest actions rather than their meanings; unrecognized retrospective distortion; and decreased naturalness in the analyst's behavior caused by efforts to present a certain image to the analysand. To the extent that analytic work became characterized by moralistic, authoritarian, or purist attitudes, it embodied features of infantile judgmental images of the parents.

There are also instances in which the principles of abstinence and neutrality and related techniques drift from afferent roles to efferent ones. For example, Lipton (1977) cited one author who considered it the analyst's role to enforce the patient's "pledge" not to rise from the couch during sessions, and another who construed analytic neutrality not only as an observational vantage point, but as "protect[ing] the patient from an objective relationship with the analyst" (p. 258). As with the "real relationship" and "empathy," exaggerated emphasis on abstinence and "basic model technique" "tends to move technique from collaboration to unilaterality" (Lipton, 1977, p. 262), distorts concepts that were developed to facilitate analyzing transference, and may impede transference analysis.

Discussion

When he developed his theories and methods, Freud held up a flickering and inconsistent candle of reason to illuminate the darkness of the unconscious. Subsequent psychoanalysts have tried to brighten that light, also with inconsistent results. One source of that inconsistency lies in the fact that psychoanalytic practice and theory-making are regularly interpreted and shaped by the unconscious fantasies of analysts and patients. I have advanced evidence that the deeply divisive controversy about the role of nontransference factors in the patient-analyst relationship is partly a consequence of such unrecognized "background" factors.

The controversy about the analytic relationship is not resolved by introducing theories that identify new nontransference elements, or that attempt to restate and reinforce the basic model technique in order to prevent difficulties and iatrogenic problems. Because such theories typically refer to manifest features of the analyst-patient relationship, they are themselves vulnerable to being assimilated to underlying conflicts, and in turn becoming converted into expressions of these. When technical guidelines are reified into rules or "factors" that are deemed to have their effects at the level of manifest behavior, they are automatically moved out of the realm of psychoanalytic understanding, out of what might be called the sphere of the analytic ego, and into the purview of the unconscious.

I have tried to add new elements to prior formulations about the influence of unconscious fantasies on theory: Whereas earlier writers have tended to emphasize instinctual, wish-fulfilling aspects of unconscious fantasies, I have stressed the defensive functions of the fantasies and of the theories to which they give rise. This approach makes the intensity, divisiveness, and persistence of theoretical controversies about the relationship more comprehensible. It also makes clear that, as defenses, these fantasies inevitably tend to distort technique in ways that impede efforts to recognize and understand unconscious conflict. I have described a characteristic alteration of concepts that occurs under the influence of the background fantasies and called it "conceptual drift."

Because conceptual drift is not limited to any school or theory, the controversies about the analytic relationship I have been discussing are best understood when both sides are considered as a unit, reflecting the different ways in which one integrated set of unconscious representations is projected onto analytic practice and theory for defensive purposes. These representations can also be projected onto concepts and onto straw men, such as fear of falling into "wild" analysis (connoting looseness and license), on one hand, and the wish to protect patients from the attitudes of "strict" Freudians and "orthodoxy," on the other. When not viewed in a unitary way but dealt with only by attempting to assess the merits or drawbacks of particular, discrete theoretical revisions or suggestions about technique, these matters have been a cause of continuing and unresolved tension, of repetitive shifts and reactive countershifts in psychoanalytic practice since its beginnings.

There are of course many sources of therapeutic gain apart from interpretation of conflict, including suggestion, identification, and other side-effects of transference and countertransference role-attributions. Although these influences are inevitable in any analysis, and they may be quite beneficial, they do not contribute directly to resolving unconscious conflicts; and in our current state of knowledge they cannot be controlled and titrated with enough accuracy to permit them to be used reliably and predictably. Following Gray (1987, 1991) I recommend that the principal psychoanalytic approach to the background fantasies described here is to study the moment-to-moment tensions in a given analysis that lead the analyst to be perceived as—or to feel inclined to behave as—a judgmental parent-figure at one time or a benevolent one at another; and then to use this understanding analytically. This task will be facilitated by following the lead of Lipton (1977), who recommended that analysts avoid theorizing about details of the relationship at a manifest level and shape their actions in light of their purposes. One such purpose is usually to keep open as many opportunities to observe and analyze conflict as possible. Beyond this, guidelines for the analyst's manifest behavior may not belong to the province of technique but merely to civility, courtesy, and ethics.

REFERENCES

Abend, S. (1979). Unconscious fantasy and theories of cure. *J. Amer. Psychoanal. Assn.*, 27:579–596.

Adler, G. (1980). Transference, real relationship and alliance. *Internat. J. Psycho-Anal.*, 61:547–558.

Arlow, J. (1981). Theories of pathogenesis. *Psychoanal. Quart.*, 50:488–514.

Dewald, P. A. (1976). Transference regression and real experience in psychoanalysis. *Psychoanal. Quart.*, 45:213–230.

Freud, S. (1912). The dynamics of transference. *S.E.*, 12.

Gray, P. (1987). On the technique of analysis of the superego—An introduction. *Psychoanal. Quart.*, 56:130–154.

______ (1991). On transferred permissive or approving superego functions: The analysis of the ego's superego activities, Part 2. *Psychoanal. Quart.*, 60:1–21.

Greenson, R. (1965). The working alliance and the transference neurosis. In: *Psychoanalytic Explorations.* New York: Int. Univ. Press, 1978, pp. 199–224.

______ (1971). The "real" relationship between patient and psychoanalyst. In: *The Unconscious Today: Essays in Honor of Max Schur,* ed. M. Kanzer. New York: Int. Univ. Press, pp. 213–232.

______ & Wexler, M. (1969). The non-transference relationship in the psychoanalytic situation. In: *Psychoanalytic Explorations.* New York: Int. Univ. Press, 1978, pp. 359–386.

Kohut, H. (1959). Introspection, empathy, and psychoanalysis. *J. Amer. Psychoanal. Assn.*, 7:459–483.

______ (1984). *How Does Analysis Cure?* ed. A. Goldberg & P. Stepansky. Chicago: Univ. Chicago Press.

Lewin, B. D. (1954). Sleep, narcissistic neurosis, and the analytic situation. *Psychoanal. Quart.*, 23:487–510.

______ (1955). Dream psychology and the analytic situation. *Psychoanal. Quart.*, 24:169–199.

Lipton, S. D. (1977). The advantages of Freud's technique as shown in his analysis of the Rat Man. *Internat. J. Psycho-Anal.*, 58:255–273.

Reed, G. (1984). The antithetical meaning of the term "empathy" in psychoanalytic discourse. In: *Empathy, I,* ed. J. Lichtenberg, M. Bornstein & D. Silver. Hillsdale, NJ: The Analytic Press, pp. 7–24.

Shapiro, T. (1981). Empathy: A critical reevaluation. *Psychoanal. Inq.,* 1:423–448.

Stone, L. (1961). *The Psychoanalytic Situation.* New York: Int. Univ. Press.

Strachey, J. (1934). The nature of the therapeutic action of psycho-analysis. *Internat. J. Psycho-Anal.,* 15:127–159.

Viederman, M. (1991). The real person of the analyst and his role in the process of psychoanalytic cure. *J. Amer. Psychoanal. Assn.,* 39:451–489.

2510 Medical Tower Building
255 South 17th Street
Philadelphia, PA 19103

Is Love in the Analytic Relationship "Real"?

AXEL HOFFER, M.D.

IN HIS ANALYSIS OF DORA, FREUD (1905, p. 116) wondered: "What are transferences?" His answer—"They are new editions or facsimiles"—raises questions highly relevant to recent shifts in psychoanalytic theory and technique. In what follows I consider three related questions:

Are positive transference and countertransference feelings imitations of true loving feelings or are they real?

What is the difference between a loving analytic relationship and an ordinary loving relationship?

What is the nature of the tension created in the analyst by the opposing tendencies of the relatively anonymous asymmetry in the analytic relationship and the self-revealing mutuality in an ordinary loving relationship?

Two quotations from Freud are immediately relevant: In discussing the analyst's response to the intense transference love of a female patient for a male analyst, he (1914) said: "It is, therefore, just as disastrous for the analysis if the patient's craving for love is gratified as if it is suppressed. The course the analyst must pursue is neither of these; it is one for which there *is no model* in real life" (p. 166). Two years later, in the context of neurotic symptom formation, Freud (1916–1917) wrote, *"it is psychical reality which is the decisive kind"* (p. 368).

The first quotation, in which Freud says that the analytic

Dr. Hoffer is a member of the faculty at the Psychoanalytic Institute of New England, East; he is a Supervising Analyst at the Massachusetts Institute of Psychoanalysis and Assistant Clinical Professor of Psychiatry, Harvard Medical School.

relationship is so different from other kinds that no model exists for it in real life, is indeed a strong statement. Could it be true? How ironic that the analyst is experienced in the transference as though he were any number of people—hence models—in the analysand's life, and yet there is no model for the analyst. On reflection, Freud's statement becomes more profound because we can recognize that in being *all* of those people for the analysand, he was also *none* of them. He was only the analyst, doing analysis. There *is* no model for the analyst in real life.

We now try to answer the first part of the first question: "Are positive transference and countertransference feelings only imitations of true loving feelings or are they real?" If we follow Freud's assertion in the second quotation that the decisive reality is psychical reality, then love is love, no matter where we find it. Is it possible to make a distinction between transference love and other kinds of love? Freud concluded that the only difference between "real" love outside of analysis and "transference" love can be found in the setting in which it arises. It serves as a resistance to remembering and hence to the work of the analysis.

In Freud's (1914) words:

> can we truly say that the state of being in love which becomes manifest in analytic treatment is not a real one? . . . We have no right to dispute that the state of being in love which makes its appearance in the course of analytic treatment has the character of "genuine" love. If it seems so lacking in normality, this is sufficiently explained by the fact that being in love in ordinary life, outside analysis, is also more similar to abnormal than normal mental phenomena [p. 168].

Expanding on the subject, Freud asserts:

> He must take care not to steer away from the transference-love, or to repulse it or to make it distasteful to the patient; but he must just as resolutely withhold any response to it. He must keep firm hold of the transference-love, but treat it as something unreal, as a situation which has to be gone through in the treatment and traced back to its unconscious origins and which

> must assist in bringing all that is most deeply hidden in the patient's erotic life into her consciousness and therefore under her control [p. 166].

And Freud concludes: "it is quite out of the question for the analyst to give way. However highly he may prize love he must prize even more highly the opportunity for helping his patient over a decisive stage in her life" (p. 170).

By "giving way," we understand Freud to refer to actions on the analyst's part which would gratify the transference wishes, thereby precluding the opportunity to analyze them.

Thus, Freud recognizes that transference love has the quality of genuine love, yet advices that we treat it as unreal. Isn't Freud hedging here as he says on the one hand transference and ordinary love are both real and abnormal, yet on the other hand that we must *treat* transference love as something "unreal"? Freud is clearly struggling as he tries to understand love in the analytic relationship. What makes the question of the reality or unreality of love in the therapeutic relationship such a difficult one with which to grapple?

From the beginnings of psychoanalysis, love, libido, and Eros have played major roles in psychoanalytic theory and technique. As early as 1906, in a letter to Jung (McGuire, 1974, pp. 12–13) Freud writes: "Transference provides the impulse necessary for understanding and translating the language of the ucs. . . . Essentially, one might say, the cure is effected by love."

Freud is here describing the importance of the patient's love of the analyst, in contrast to Ferenczi's emphasis in the late twenties and early thirties in his technique (1930) of "relaxation" and "indulgence" on the importance of the *analyst's* genuine love for the patient. More recently, psychoanalytic attention has focused in a more even-handed way on the feelings of both analyst and analysand. The construction of reality by the analyst as well as by the patient has been emphasized (see, for example, Modell, 1990). A review of the shifts in psychoanalytic theory and technique from the sixties into the eighties will put the question of the "reality" of love in the analytic relationship into clearer perspective. The shifts in psychoanalytic practice also reflect societal shifts away from authoritarianism and certainty toward egalitarianism and relativity. I will illustrate these shifts by comparing Greenson's (1967) analytic practice in the sixties first with Sandor Ferenczi's technique back in the thirties (1931) and then forward to the present with my views on psychoanalytic neutrality (1985).

Greenson (1967, pp. 152–153) states:

> Transference reactions are always inappropriate. They may be so in the quality, quantity, or duration of the reaction. One may overreact or underreact, or one may have a bizarre reaction to the transference object. The transference reaction is unsuitable in its current context; but it was once an appropriate reaction to a past situation. Just as ill-fitting as transference reactions are to a person in the present, they fit snugly to someone in the past. For example, a young woman patient reacts to my keeping her waiting for two or three minutes by becoming tearful and angry, fantasying that I must be giving extra time to my favorite woman patient. This is an inappropriate reaction in a thirty-five-year-old intelligent and cultured woman, but her associations lead to a past situation where this set of feelings and fantasies fit. She recalls her reactions as a child of five waiting for her father to come to her room to kiss her good night. She always had to wait a few minutes because he made it a rule to kiss her younger sister good night first. Then she reacted by tears, anger, and jealousy fantasies—precisely what she is now experiencing with me. Her reactions are appropriate for a five-year-old girl, but obviously not fitting for a thirty-five-year-old woman. The key to understanding this behavior is recognizing that it is a repetition of the past, i.e., a transference reaction.

I agree with part of what Greenson says here, namely, the usefulness of pursuing the patient's associations to the analyst's lateness to deepen our understanding of the psychic reality of the past. But referring to the transference reaction as "inappropiate" implies a perjorative judgment. Being an analytic patient is difficult enough without having to bear the humiliation of the analyst's judging which of her reactions are "childish and inappropriate" and which are "reasonable." Is such a judgment necessary to our work? In my view, it is not only unnecessary but detrimental. Such judgments distract the analyst and analysand from attending to the patient's psychic reality if both become preoccupied with judging whether a particular response to him is realistic or not, childish or not, inappropriate or not, hence, transference or not.

It is therefore particularly noteworthy that as early as 1931, Ferenczi was already arguing for a focus on the patient's psychic reality. He stated:

> it is advantageous; to consider for a time *every one,* even the most improbable, of the communications as in some way possible, even to accept an apparently obvious delusion. Two reasons for this: thus, by leaving aside the "reality" question, one can feel one's way more completely into the patient's mental life. (Here something should be said about the disadvantages of contrasting "reality" and "unreality." The latter must in any case be taken equally seriously as a *psychic* reality; hence above all one must become fully absorbed in all that the patient says and feels [p. 235].

I have attempted elsewhere (Hoffer, 1985) to resolve the problem of the analyst's judgment by reformulating the concept of neutrality in terms of the analyst's position in relation to specifiable conflicts of the patient. I emphasize the inherent respect for the patient's autonomy contained in the analyst's honest suspension of judgment about how a patient should resolve his or her conflicts. Even though common usage of the term neutrality has given it a bad name as implying coldness, distance, or indifference on the analyst's part, I submit that a position of genuine neutrality in relation to fully exploring the patient's conflicts—not how they "should" be resolved—*is* actively loving and involved. Indeed, differing with the commonly held view that neutrality is antithetical to empathy, I believe genuine neutrality in relation to the patient's conflicts is an essential ingredient of the analyst's empathy. I have frequently observed that examples presented to me by supervisees as "a failure of empathy" are more usefully understood as "an abandonment of neutrality" regarding a particular conflict (see also Schwaber, 1992). The analyst's awareness of even a slight pull away from a neutral position in relation to a conflict can serve as an early warning signal of countertransference intrusion.

I therefore suggest that transference and countertransference—the latter defined by McLaughlin (1981) as the analyst's transference to the patient—are as real and genuine as any other feelings. Furthermore, as already noted, the analyst's efforts to distinguish between "real" and "transference," "appropriate" and "inappropriate," "childish" and "mature" feelings serve as distractions. They are distractions from and resistances to listening to the patient in order to deepen our understanding of who the patient really is and where the patient lives, namely, in his or her psychic reality.

For purposes of this discussion, I would underscore that the phenomena of transference feelings and countertransference feelings occur all the time in all relationships (see Greenson, 1965; Brenner, 1979). The crucial difference is that in analysis, these feelings are the object of focused inquiry and are given names for heuristic reasons. The point is that the feelings are real—they are not imitations—wherever they occur and whatever names they are given. Indeed, excessive efforts at naming them can diminish our appreciation of their reality!

Let us proceed now from the discussion of the reality of the loving feelings to two areas that distinguish love in the therapeutic relationship from love in ordinary relationships: equality and mutuality. We have already touched on the issue of inequality when the analyst views himself as the judge, arbiter, or knower. In the following clinical vignette, Greenson's (1967) comment calls our attention to an important point bearing directly on our discussion of equality and mutuality:

> A young woman, shy and timid, begins in the third month of her analysis to evince unmistakable signs of believing she had fallen in love with me. Finally, after some days of struggling with her feelings, she tearfully confesses her love. Then she begs me not to treat this state of affairs in the same cold, analytic way I had treated her other emotions. She pleads with me not to remain silent and aloof. I should please say something, any-

> thing—it is so humiliating for her to be in such a position. She weeps and sobs and becomes silent. After a while I say, "I know this is very hard for you, but it is important for us that you try to express exactly how you feel." The patient is silent a moment and then says pleadingly and angrily: "It's not fair, you can hide behind the analytic couch, and I have to expose all. I know you don't love me, but at least tell me if you like me; admit you care a little, tell me I'm not just a number to you—the eleven o'clock patient." She weeps and sobs and is silent again. I too keep silent for a time and then say: "It's true, it is not fair; the analytic situation is not an equal one; it is your task to let your feelings come out and it is my job to understand you, to analyze what comes up. Yes, it's not fair [pp. 226–227].

For purposes of analyzing this patient, in my view, it would be more useful analytically to explore the ways in which the patient experienced the analyst as unfair than to comment on the "truth" versus "nontruth" of it. For purposes of this discussion, however, let us shift our focus and use Greenson's comment as a springboard to contemplate the inherent "unfairness" to which he refers. I submit that love in an analytic relationship—whether or not we call it transference and countertransference—is the same and as real as ordinary love outside of therapy. The difference is not to be found in its reality but in its unique one-sidedness. On the analyst's part, the loving relationship is one-sided because of its purpose—namely, that the raison d'être of the relationship is that it exists for the patient's benefit. That, after all, is why the patient is in analysis. Moreover, the analytic setting, context, and frame are naturally defined by and subordinate to its purpose. Therefore, although the analyst and patient may "really" love each other, the relationship is not equal and thus not mutual in the ordinary sense.

In my view, considering the feelings in an analytic relationship as less "real" than in an ordinary relationship creates a false and misleading dichotomy. The uniqueness of the analytic relationship lies in its purpose and unilateral focus. It exists for the benefit of the patient; it offers growth and self-understanding—especially of unconscious processes—through the medium of the relationship with the analyst. It is a paradoxical uniqueness because it is like every other relationship, yet unlike any other. The intimacy implicit in saying anything and everything that comes to mind provides the analyst with a unique privilege and an awesome responsibility.

There are of course many types of relationships that are growth-promoting and therapeutic. In addition to psychoanalysts who are supposed to be therapeutic, there is much that may be considered therapeutic in virtually all relationships, ranging from an inspiring teacher to a bartender with a good ear. Finally, it goes without saying that I am not suggesting that the analyst is an altruistic saint who does not benefit from the relationship. In addition to being paid, the analyst enjoys, learns, and grows from his work. A dentist also works for the patient's benefit but he uses his hands and his instruments—not himself—therapeutically. What is different and unique here is that the analytic relationship itself is the focus of and focused on the patient's treatment.

Loving a teacher, especially having a crush on a teacher, can inspire a student to learn. A wish to please and an identification with a beloved teacher have provided the impetus for many successful careers. Freud recognized the importance of such feelings in providing motivation for treatment (McGuire, 1974, p. 13). He called them the basis for the "unobjectionable positive transference." That term is the forerunner of Zetzel's (1956) concept of the therapeutic alliance and Greenson's (1965) concept of the working alliance. On the other hand, Freud was very mindful of the potential short-circuiting of the work of therapy through suggestion or by means of a transference cure, where the patient's symptoms improve temporarily as a result of the temporary idealization of the analyst.

The tension created by the opposing tendencies of asymmetry and mutuality can now be considered. Efforts to dissolve the asymmetrical analytic relationship and replace it with another kind of relationship, one which is mutual and equal, are universal. These universal efforts—present at various times in both patient and analyst—create a "normal" tension, but understood as a resistance to the work of analysis. This essential tension, arising from the natural tendency to transform the unequal analytic relationship into an equal and mutual one, is to be found to varying degrees in every analysis. Heightened awareness of the universality of that tension can help us think more clearly about love in the analytic relationship.

Two historical facts will now be described and then used as a metaphor for the feelings, conflicts, and consequent tensions with which each analyst must deal in daily work. The first is Ferenczi's long-standing pressure on Freud to engage in a more mutual relationship with him. The second is Ferenczi's radical experiment with "mutual analysis." From the beginning, Freud had a terrible time with love in psychoanalysis. He early viewed love as explosive, thus potentially dangerous to the psychoanalytic enterprise. For example, as early as June, 1909, in reply to Jung's letter describing his sexual involvement with his analysand, Sabina Spielrein, Freud (McGuire, 1974) writes:

> Such experiences, though painful, are necessary and hard to avoid. Without them we cannot really know life and what we are dealing with. I myself have never been taken in quite so badly, but I have come very close to it a number of times and had a *narrow escape* [English in the original]. I believe that only grim necessities weighing on my work, and the fact that I was ten years older than yourself when I came to psyA, have saved me from similar experiences. But no lasting harm is done. They help us to develop the thick skin we need and to dominate "countertransference," which is after all a permanent problem for us; they teach us to displace our own affects to best advantage. They are a *"blessing in disguise"* [pp. 230–231, English in the original].

Freud's recommendation that Jung develop a thick skin is very revealing. In sharp contrast to Freud, Ferenczi devoted himself to removing any emotional wall separating himself from his analysands. Can one be an effective analyst with a thick skin? With a thin skin? How thick should the good analyst's skin be?

It is noteworthy that in this 1909 letter to Jung,[1] Freud used the

[1] I wish to thank Drs. Haynal and Falzeder for calling my attention to the Freud-Jung letters cited.

term countertransference for the first time. In his paper on transference-love, Freud (1914) continues in the same vein:

> The psycho-analyst knows that he is working with highly explosive forces and that he needs to proceed with as much caution and conscientiousness as a chemist. But when have chemists ever been forbidden, because of the danger, from handling explosive substances, which are indispensable, on account of their effects? . . . psycho-analysis . . . is not afraid to handle the most dangerous mental impulses and to obtain mastery over them for the benefit of the patient [p. 170].

As a final illustration of the problem of mutuality in psychoanalysis, the Freud-Ferenczi relationship provides numerous significant and dramatic examples (Hoffer, 1991). Ferenczi was Freud's most beloved student and follower, his analysand for three brief periods, one in 1914 and two in 1916. Their extensive correspondence, beginning in 1908 and ending with Ferenczi's death of pernicious anemia in 1933, movingly documents their love for one another. Freud's analysis of Ferenczi is complicated by the blurring of their personal, professional, and analytic relationships; they were teacher-student, friends, colleagues, confidants, traveling companions, as well as analyst-analysand. But already in 1913, long before the analysis for which Ferenczi pleaded, Freud prophetically wrote (Dupont, in press): "There is another consideration which comes into play: my disinclination to expose one of my most indispensible assistants to the danger of a personal estrangement because of the analysis" (p. 10).

Unlike Ferenczi, Freud views the analytic relationship as one which can be more or less encapsulated and contained in the analytic hour. Thus, for Freud "the analysis" occurs only in the designated hours. This view explains how Freud could analyze his daughter, Anna—twice—while living with her, without his feelings having both a personal and an analytic relationship as an insurmountable strain. As Dupont (in press) reports, Freud could analyze Ferenczi anywhere—even on vacation. Freud writes to Ferenczi: "I will save you . . . two sessions a day. I hope that we will see much of you besides; I would hope that you can take at least one meal with us every day. Technique will demand, however, that outside of the session, nothing personal will be entered into" (p. 25).

It is hard for us to imagine (or perhaps not so hard) actually going on vacation with our analyst during the analysis. Yet Freud was comfortable with doing it, so long as "nothing personal is entered into" outside the hours. Does analysis occur only in the analytic hour? What does this statement tell us about Freud's view of the analytic relationship? Indeed, by means of this kind of compartmentalization, wherein the analytic hour was analogous to a surgical operating room with aseptic "technique" focused on the analytic task and the analysis of dreams and transference. Freud was able to analyze his daughter. And presumably by similar means he was able to analyze—albeit reluctantly—his favorite pupil, Ferenczi, whom he addressed as "Dear son," and who, after Jung's defection, he viewed as the "Crown Prince of psychoanalysis" (Dupont, in press).

Unfortunately, in the late nineteen-twenties, the intimate and loving relationship between Freud and Ferenczi was torn apart by disagreements which caused a profound upheaval not only in their personal relationship but also in the entire psychoanalytic community. As late as 1930, Freud expressed dismay at Ferenczi's trying to push Freud into resuming the analysis in order to complete it. Freud had no interest in trying to make up for what was missed in the past, urging that it be left to Ferenczi's self-analysis. Ferenczi's response in February, 1930 conveys the flavor of their exchange:

> The analytically open exchange in no way means that I want to push you into the role of analyst again and thereby give you up as a tried and tested, proven friend. My hope—which I believe is not unjustified—is that an analytically free exchange is also possible between reliable friends. I must confess that I would no longer feel right in the one-sided role of analysand. Do you think that such a mutual openness would be impossible? [quoted by permission of J. Dupont; my translation].

The history of the Freud-Ferenczi relationship contains many more expressions of Ferenczi's desire for a mutual, egalitarian relationship with Freud. Indeed, in 1926, Ferenczi offered to analyze Freud, but the offer was declined (Dupont, in press). Understanding that history, we need not be surprised by the following description of Ferenczi's most radical technical experiment. As he tells us in his *Clinical Diary* (1932; Hoffer, 1990), Ferenczi was pressed by a severely traumatized patient in a stalemated analysis openly to acknowledge with her his unresolved countertransference difficulties. The patient ("RN") felt strongly that the only honest way to continue the analysis beyond their stalemate was for Ferenczi to agree to be analyzed by her. With his characteristic openness, his egalitarian tendencies, his willingness to take personal risks and to experiment, and out of desperation, Ferenczi consented to reverse roles and position. For a period of several months, Ferenczi and RN take turns sitting behind the couch, a procedure Ferenczi called "mutual analysis." Ferenczi (1932, p. 56) describes it as follows:

> Certain phases of mutual analysis represent the complete renunciation of all compulsion and of all authority on both sides: they give the impression of two equally terrified children who compare their experiences, and because of their common fate understand each other completely and instinctively try to comfort each other. Awareness of this shared fate allows the partner to appear as completely harmless, therefore as someone whom one can trust with confidence.

Although Ferenczi concluded that the technique of mutual analysis permitted this analysis to proceed to a successful outcome, his explicit reason for stopping the experiment was his practical concern about maintaining the confidentiality of his other patients. He realized that if he truly said everything that came to mind, he would reveal the confidences of his other patients to this patient. While I have a respectful appreciation of the dilemma Ferenczi was facing and of his wish to be honest to help the patient feel safe, I want to be clear that I do not recommend mutual analysis. Furthermore, I feel strongly that a countertransference problem is the analyst's problem for which the analyst must take responsibility while attending to its impact on the patient. It is not a mutual problem, and the purpose of analysis is not to provide mutual comfort. Finally, I doubt whether genuine free association is possible in such a mutual analysis (Rizzuto, personal communication); countertransference confession, yes; but free association, no.

But what relevance can this radical experiment, which Ferenczi himself subsequently renounced, possibly have to today's analyst? I propose there is much for us to learn from the historical fact of "mutual analysis" when viewed as a metaphor for feelings, conflicts, and tensions which analysts and analysands universally feel but which Ferenczi actually acted upon. Ferenczi's relentless pressure on Freud for a mutual relationship and his brief experiment with mutual analysis pose challenges to Freud's principles of maintaining analytic abstinence and the analyst's relative anonymity. The historical facts illustrate the complex problems created by the blurring of personal and professional relationships. And of particular usefulness is our opportunity to view the painful struggles of Freud and Ferenczi as a metaphor in our daily work demonstrating the powerful pulls—often not clearly recognized—toward equality and mutuality. Thus, the metaphor of mutual analysis brightly illuminates an insufficiently recognized universal wish of the analyst to make his role a complementary one, turning the necessarily asymmetrical, analytic relationship into a mutual, ordinary one. Furthermore, this metaphor highlights the inevitable tension arising from the analyst's struggle with and against a mutual relationship with the analysand.[2] Heightening awareness of the existence of this constant tension in the analyst constitutes an important aspect of self-analytic work.

To recapitulate, attempting now to answer the questions posed at the beginning of this paper, we may conclude that the positive feelings between analyst and analysand are real, not imitations; the difference between an analytic relationship and an ordinary one lies in its inherent purpose, namely, that the former exists—asymmetrically—for the benefit of the patient. Thus defined by its purpose, the analytic relationship is not mutual. However, the pull

[2]Elucidation of (1) how each analyst uniquely and optimally deals with that tension, (2) those features of mutuality specific to the analytic relationship, and (3) the connection between mutuality and the concept of therapeutic alliance lies beyond the scope of this paper (Hoffer, 1992).

on both analyst and analysand to transform the analytic relationship into an ordinary, self-revealing, mutual one, as exemplified by Ferenczi's wish to analyze Freud and by his experiment with mutual analysis, creates an inevitable and necessary tension in the analyst. The importance of the analyst's awareness of that tension is highlighted.

REFERENCES

Brenner, C. (1979). Working alliance, therapeutic alliance, and transference. *J. Amer. Psychoanal. Assn.*, 27:137–158.

Dupont, J. (in press). Freud's analysis of Ferenczi as revealed in their correspondence. *Internat. J. Psycho-Anal.*

Ferenczi, S. (1930). On the theme of neocatharsis. In: *Final Contributions to the Problems and Methods of Psycho-analysis.* New York: Basic Books, 1955, pp. 223–224.

______ (1931). On the patient's initiative. In: *Final Contributions to the Problems and Methods of Psycho-analysis.* New York: Basic Books, 1955, p. 235.

______ (1932). *The Clinical Diary of Sándor Ferenczi,* ed. J. Dupont. Cambridge: Harvard Univ. Press, 1988.

Freud, S. (1905). Fragment of an analysis of a case of hysteria. *S.E.*, 7.

______ (1914). Observations on transference-love. *S.E.*, 12.

______ (1916–1917). Introductory lectures on psycho-analysis. *S.E.*, 16.

Greenson, R. (1965). The working alliance and the transference neuroses. In: *Explorations in Psychoanalysis.* New York: Int. Univ. Press, 1978, pp. 199–224.

______ (1967). *The Technique and Practice of Psychoanalysis.* New York: Int. Univ. Press.

Hoffer, A. (1965). Toward a definition of psychoanalytic neutrality. *J. Amer. Psychoanal. Assn.*, 33(4):771–795.

______ (1990). Book Review: *The Clinical Diary of Sándor Ferenczi,* ed. J. Dupont. *Internat. J. Psycho-Anal.*, 71(4):723–727.

______ (1991). The Freud-Ferenczi controversy—A living legacy. *Internat. Rev. Psycho-Anal.*, 18(4):465–472.

______ (1992). Asymétrie et mutualité dans la relation analytique: Leçons actuelles des rapports entre Freud-Ferenczi. Paris: Le Coq-Héron.

McGuire, W., ed. (1974). *The Freud–Jung Letters.* Princeton: Princeton Univ. Press.

McLaughlin, J. (1981). Transference, psychic reality, and countertransference. *Psychoanal. Quart.*, 50:639–664.

Modell, A. (1990). Confusion of tongues or whose reality is it? In: *Other Times, Other Realities.* Cambridge, MA: Harvard Univ. Press.

Schwaber, E. A. (1992). Countertransference: The analyst's retreat from the patient's vantage point. *Internat. J. Psycho-Anal.*, 73:349–362.

Zetzel, E. (1956). Current concepts of transference. *Internat. J. Psycho-Anal.*, 37:369–378.

14 Welland Road
Brookline, MA 02146

Slaying the Dragons of the Past or Cooking the Hare in the Present: A Historical View on Affects in the Psychoanalytic Encounter

ANDRÉ HAYNAL, M.D.
ERNST FALZEDER, Ph.D.

WHILE WE WOULD ALL AGREE that transference is of central importance to psychoanalytic treatment, it remains a matter of continuing controversy as to how much and in what ways the phenomena described with this term are to be attributed to present "reality" or to past "illusion." In his earliest formulations, Freud tied these affective manifestations to the patient's past. However, this view—which in retrospect may be seen as covertly containing a distancing maneuver included for the comfort of the analyst—did not represent a satisfactory or definitive solution to all of the difficulties present. Ultimately, Freud developed a complex position: on the one hand, he continued to see transference feelings as "new editions" of old "facsimiles" (1905, p. 116); on the other hand, he not only acknowledged the actuality of these feelings, but saw them as an important tool for change within the treatment.

The nature of the actual, ongoing interactions between

André E. Haynal is Professor of Psychiatry and Medical Psychology and Chairman of the Department of Psychiatry, University of Geneva, former President of the Swiss Psychoanalytic Society, former Vice-President of the European Psychoanalytic Federation, and former visiting professor at Stanford University.

Ernst Falzeder is a research fellow at the Balint Archives (Geneva, Switzerland), lecturer at the University of Salzburg (Austria), and coeditor of the Sigmund Freud/Sándor Ferenczi correspondence.

analysand and analyst and the feelings and experiences that these gave rise to later became the subject of intense investigation and lively exchange between Freud and members of his circle. Ferenczi, in particular, assumed a leading role in expanding upon Freud's original ideas. Although some of Ferenczi's innovative concepts—such as a deepened appreciation of the interactive dimension of the analytic relationship, the fundamental importance of the analyst's feelings as a tool for understanding the evolution of the psychoanalytic process, and the role of the mother in determining the transference—were accepted by an important part of the psychoanalytic community, often without explicit acknowledgment of their origin, others, such as mutual analysis and the revival of childhood trauma during analysis, were disparaged or rejected. This negative response followed Freud's expressing his ambivalence and the opposition of important members of his circle (e.g., Abraham and Jones) toward some of these ideas. Over time, however, Ferenczi's ideas have progressively resurfaced in contemporary descriptions and theories of the therapeutic encounter. It therefore seems appropriate for us to attempt to trace these ideas back to their origin and examine, in the historical context, their early elaboration and the conflicts that have surrounded them almost from their inception.

In considering his early psychotherapeutic experience, Freud wrote (Breuer and Freud, 1893–1895) that "it is almost inevitable that [the patients'] personal relation to [the therapist] will force itself . . . unduly into the foreground" (p. 266) and that this relationship can even become "the worst obstacle that we can come across." But it cannot be avoided because one "can . . . reckon on meeting it in every comparatively serious analysis" (p. 301).

Freud already feels that he is working in the shade of affects: the "procedure . . . presupposes . . . personal concern for the patients. . . . I cannot imagine bringing myself to delve into the psychical mechanism of a hysteria in anyone who . . . would not be capable of arousing human sympathy" (p. 265). Moreover, this sympathy is also demanded by the patients—who view their cooperation as "a personal sacrifice, which must be compensated by some substitute for love" (p. 301).

Yet, very early, Freud encounters love not only in this mild "substitute" form, but also in its full affective implications—thus becoming a disturbance. In this context let us evoke his well-known report, according to which a patient "threw her arms around my neck" and only the "unexpected entrance of a servant relieved us from a painful discussion" (1925, p. 27). A proof of love, it seems, on the motives of which Freud pondered, however: "I was modest enough not to attribute the event to my own irresistible personal attraction," but to the *past* of the subject. In linking the patients' emotions with the past, he saw them as a *"false connection"* (1893–1895, p. 302) and thus came to conceptualize the notion of transference.

As far as Freud's reaction to the theme of sexuality is concerned, we find that remarkable report in "The Psychopathology of Everyday Life" that "a young girl . . . aroused a feeling of pleasure in me which I had long thought was extinct." By an "apparently clumsy movement," he continues, "I suddenly found myself standing directly behind her, and throwing my arms round her from behind; and for a moment my hands met in front of her waist" (1901, p. 176).[1]

In the discussion of the Dora case (1905) he confessed his vulnerability: "No one who, like me, conjures up the most evil of those half-tamed demons that inhabit the human breast, and seeks to wrestle with them, can expect to come through the struggle unscathed" (p. 109). It is here that Freud fully recognized his failure to have considered affective implications: "I was deaf to this first note of warning" (p. 119). We can only speculate, as Decker (1991) does, that Freud might have been sexually aroused by this young woman, who spoke to him about her sexual temptations during the treatment. In any case, to conceal his embarrassment, he found it necessary to make an apologetic explanation in a foreign language about being able to discuss sexual matters with a young lady: *"J'appelle un chat un chat"* (p. 48) and: *"pour faire une omelette il faut casser des oeufs"*[2] (p. 49).

[1]The original German *"vor ihrem Schoss"* (*G. W. IV*, p. 195) would be more properly translated as "in front of her lap" or even "in front of her genitals" (*Schoss* being also a widespread euphemism for the female genitals), either of which would better account for his embarrassment.

[2]See also Freud's turning to Spanish as an "official language" in his adolescent letters to Silberstein (Boelich, 1990, p. 11), when he writes to his friend about another deeply personal matter, this time his feelings for Gisella Fluss.

Freud evidently took a parental stance and recognized too late that it was again "transference" that led to the failure of the treatment.

But Freud was also implicated in other experiences of overinvolvement, related to him by his closest collaborators and friends: Breuer, Jung, and Ferenczi.

With Breuer

The first of these incidents where love was triggered in the therapeutic situation and was transformed to passion and obviously could not be mastered, was between Anna O, Breuer, and Freud himself. Even if this encounter was to become, later on, the object of legend (Breuer breaking off the treatment in panic and leaving with his wife for a second honeymoon to Venice, there procreating his last child), the whole affair was, without any doubt, unsettling enough (cf. Hirschmüller, 1978, pp. 170–178). All this seemed so important to Freud that he did not hesitate to declare in the opening phrases of the first of the Clark lectures that the "merit to have brought psycho-analysis into being" (1910, p. 9) had to be attributed to Dr. Breuer and his patient (Bertha Pappenheim).

Breuer, for his part, in recalling the case of Anna O, wrote in a letter to Auguste Forel from November 21, 1907, that he had "learned . . . that a 'general practitioner' [in English in the German text] cannot treat such a case without being totally destroyed in his activities and life style. I had by that time sworn never to go through such an ordeal again" (Ackerknecht, 1957, p. 170; our translation).

Decades later, Ferenczi wrote about that time in his *Clinical Diary* (1932) that Freud "followed Breuer with enthusiasm (if necessary spending hours lying on the floor next to a person in a hysterical crisis). He must have been first shaken and then disenchanted, however, by certain experiences, rather like Breuer when his patient had a relapse and when the problem of countertransference opened up before him like an abyss. This may well correspond in Freud's case to the discovery that hysterics lie. Since making this discovery Freud no longer loves his patients" (p. 93).

After the triangular situation with Breuer and Anna O, Freud was to find himself—as far as we know—on at least two more occasions, involved in similar situations in transference-triggered love affairs: between Sabina Spielrein and Jung (1908–1909) and, a few years later, between Elma Pálos and Ferenczi (1911–1912).

With Jung

The correspondence between Freud and Jung begins (all quotations are from McGuire, 1974), as in a Greek tragedy with a seemingly insignificant statement, which is nevertheless a sign of future trouble: "I am currently treating an hysteric with your method," writes Jung. "Difficult case, a 20-year-old Russian girl student, ill for 6 years" (p. 7). In the course of the treatment, Jung falls in love with this patient but does not tell Freud so. It is only three years later, in 1909, that he alludes to this fact, still in a very hypocritical manner: "a woman patient, whom years ago I pulled out of a very sticky neurosis with unstinting effort, has violated my confidence and my friendship in the most mortifying way imaginable. She has kicked up a vile scandal solely because I denied myself the pleasure of giving her a child." He insists—falsely—that "I have always acted the gentleman towards her," but at the same time speaks of having discovered his "polygamous components" (p. 207).

Already in 1906 Freud had recognized, in a letter to Jung, that analysis is "actually a healing through love" (p. 13; our translation), and he repeated the same statement a month later before the Viennese Psychoanalytic Society (Nunberg and Federn, 1962, p. 101). On January 19, 1908, he wrote to Abraham: "Back to technique.[3] You are right, that was the most taxing of all to acquire, and that is why I want to spare those who follow in my footsteps part of the grind and—part of the cost" (Abraham and

[3]In the intellectual milieu of Freud's Vienna, the term *technique* connoted the technique of the arts—i.e., of the pianist or painter—rather than that of technology, as we might understand it today. During Freud's lifetime, the first of Hippocrates' aphorisms: *"Ho bios brakhus, he de techne makra"* (in Latin: *"ars longa, vita brevis"*) was quite common, especially among students of medicine, for whom "techne" = "art." Hence, the technique of psychoanalysis is the *art* of psychoanalysis, as opposed to the theory.

Freud, 1965, p. 24). Easter 1908 was the time of the meeting in Salzburg, where Freud presented the case of the Rat Man, speaking for five hours without interruption, moved by the desire to convey what preoccupied him. He had, as he wrote in another context to Abraham, "to recuperate from psycho-analysis by working, otherwise I should not be able to stand it" (Abraham and Freud, 1965, p. 120), and to Ferenczi: "All time long I have been depressed and narcotized myself by writing—writing—writing" (Brabant et al., 1992, letter of 2.1.1912).

This state of mind has its origin in the affective mobilization of the analyst (cf. McGuire, 1974, pp. 210–221), driving Freud to grasp the importance of the analyst's feelings. On December 26, 1908, he writes to Abraham that "It has often been my experience that just those cases in which I took an excessive personal interested failed, perhaps just because of the intensity of feeling" (Abraham and Freud, 1965, p. 63). Abraham, for his part, reports to Freud the beautiful observation that he often casts a quick glance at the picture of his parents while waiting for a patient's reply. "The glance is always accompanied by a certain guilt feeling: what will they think of me?" (Abraham and Freud, 1965, p. 77).

Returning to Jung and Sabina Spielrein, it is only a few months later that Jung confesses to Freud that he "devote[d] a large measure of friendship to her" (pp. 228–229), not daring to write openly that this meant that in reality he had become her lover, no doubt in the wake of feelings mobilized during the treatment. The whole problem of love is experienced and developed in a very dramatic manner in this trio of Spielrein, an embarrassed Jung trying to justify himself, and Freud who wants to understand and at the same time exert a sort of control. He writes to Jung: "Such experiences, though painful, are necessary and hard to avoid. . . . I myself have never been taken in quite so badly, but I have come very close to it a number of times and had *a narrow escape* [in English in the original]. . . . But no lasting harm is done. They help us to develop the thick skin we need to dominate 'countertransference' . . . they teach us to displace our own affects to best advantage. They are a *blessing in disguise*" (in italics and in English in the original, pp. 230–231).

Such a conclusion, however, is not easily reached. It is remark able that he twice uses expressions in English in the quoted letter. It seems to us, as we mentioned earlier, that this reflects his difficulty in dealing with these feelings and affects. As a result of these upsetting interactions he is inclined to let the work be done by the *analysand.* With what he called the "endopsychic" solution (p. 235), the patient ought to be able to transform these experiences into another constellation—through an intrapsychic modification of feelings mobilized in the transference and through mechanisms of introjection and working through—and thus be enriched.

Freud is inclined to resort to his modal of science as a means of protection: "Remember Lassalle's fine sentence about the chemist whose test tube had cracked: 'With a slight frown over the resistance of matter, he gets on with his work' " (p. 235). Freud seems to be seeking a balance between the provoked affects and his scientific *Weltanschauung,* which might enable him to keep the analytic process on an "endopsychic" level: a love affair which ought to be able to be transformed into a matter of intellectual scrutiny and introjection.

Later, in August 1909, when Freud gives his famous lectures at Clark University, he again resorts to a scientific metaphor: the "symptoms," he states, "to take an analogy from chemistry, are precipitates of earlier experiences in the sphere of love . . . and it is only in the raised temperature of his experience of the transference that they can be resolved and reduced to other psychical products. In this reaction the physician, if I may borrow an apt phrase from Ferenczi (1909), plays the part of a catalytic ferment, which temporarily attracts to itself the affects liberated in the process" (1910, p. 51).

Upon their return to Europe, Freud and Jung continued to try to ferret out the secrets of how, and perhaps why, love and other affects are aroused in therapy and how they are communicated in part unconsciously in transference and countertransference. How disturbing this was can be guessed from Freud's remark to Jung that a paper on countertransference seemed to be "sorely needed," adding: "of course we could not publish it, we should have to circulate copies among ourselves" (McGuire, 1974, p. 476).

As far as Jung and Sabina Spielrein are concerned, we can not describe what followed in detail. Suffice to say, it seems impossible to read Sabina's letters without being touched. Like Jung's wife, Emma, and Ferenczi's wife, Gizella, Sabina Spielrein seems to have been a woman of astonishing sensitivity and great authenticity. Let us turn instead to Freud, who, on October 12, 1911, reported to Jung (p. 447) that Fräulein Spielrein "turned up unexpectedly."

Freud was profoundly affected by what happened to the man whom he considered his "heir" and public representative. However, despite this ending, the theme of love, and affects in general, in psychoanalysis did not cease to concern him—all the more in that somebody as close to him as Ferenczi was about to implicate him, in another manner, in a not dissimilar situation.

With Ferenczi

On July 14, 1911, Sándor Ferenczi wrote to Freud (the quotations in this section are taken from Brabant et al., 1992, our translations) that he had taken into analysis the daughter of his mistress Gizella Pálos,[4] Elma Pálos, who suffered a depression following the suicide of her friend. In the course of the analysis Ferenczi fell in love with Elma, who entered "victoriously into [his] heart" (3.12.11). "I could not maintain the cold superiority of the analyst with Elma," he confessed, and, at the end of that year, even mentioned the possibility of marriage.

So Ferenczi found himself in a triangle between his mistress and her young daughter, his patient, and, even worse, tormented by doubts as to whether it was a matter of "marriage or treatment of the sickness" (1.1.1912). In that same letter Ferenczi most urgently requested that Freud should take over the analysis of the young woman who had become his fiancée. "Since you request neither my inclinations nor my predictions," Freud answered, "but you *require* me to take her into analysis, I am obliged to do so" (2.1.1912). There followed a period of insecurity, of changes of decisions, although Ferenczi was aware that in rushing headlong

[4]Ferenczi had fallen in love with Gizella Pálos (1863–1949) around 1900, and had already "treated" her "analytically"—probably *during* their friendly relations (30.10.1909).

into the affair he set on stage an "adventure that . . . has brought me close to realizing my 'family romance.' "

There was, in the Freud/Ferenczi correspondence at this time, an exchange of the utmost intimacy between them, with Freud revealing quite openly the most personal details of what he had learned from his analysand Elma. Ferenczi gradually tried to distance himself from what he called his "mishap" in a letter to Freud (20.1.1912). Elma, having completed a "piece of analysis" with Freud between the New Year and Easter, 1912, returned to Ferenczi to finish her analysis. In understandably very difficult circumstances, Ferenczi had to admit that he had made a mistake. In a painful to and fro he separated from Elma, encouraged to do so by Freud. There remained within him a sadness to which he was not easily resigned and to which he perhaps never fully adjusted.

So far, we have stressed Freud's attribution of the affects, in particular, love, in the psychoanalytic encounter to the past of the other. On closer inspection, however, we find that his involvement made him take another seminal step toward recognizing that transference affects were not mere illusions. We see him still uncertain, torn between his reservations regarding the effects of an analysis of intimate relationships, being "concerned at linking the fate of our friendship with something else different and indefinable" (21.4.12), but also a deep sympathy for Ferenczi and for his and Gizella Pálos' fate. When Ferenczi asked Freud to analyze him, Freud indeed mentioned "the danger of personal alienation caused by analysis" (4.5.13), seeing the dangers more clearly than Ferenczi, but despite that he analyzed Elma, Ferenczi, and his daughter Anna twice (Young-Bruehl, 1988, pp. 80–90, 103–109, 114–116, 122–125).

In effect, Freud's position was based on two theses. First, it was undeniable for him that affectivity in analysis is fundamental. Freud maintained that the attempt to work with transferred emotions fails, "For when all is said and done, it is impossible to destroy anyone *in absentia* or *in effigie*" (1912, p. 108), and, in 1937, he uses the metaphor of *"the dragons of primaeval days"* (p. 229; our italics). Thus, when Ferenczi (and Rank) later stress the importance of *experience* in the analytic treatment, when Ferenczi states that, although the aim of the cure remains in "substituting recollection for acting out," "you must *catch the hare before you can cook him"* (1931, pp. 131–132, our italics), they pick up and further develop a line already opened by Freud himself.

Second, Freud had a somewhat protective attitude for the analyst: let us remember, for instance, his famous simile of the "surgeon, who puts aside all his feelings, even his human sympathy" (1912, p. 115), justifying this attitude with the fact that "this emotional coldness . . . creates . . . for the doctor a desirable protection for his own emotional life." He complained in a letter to Pfister about the "cross" of transference and the "unyielding stubbornness of the illness" (Meng and Freud, 1963, p. 39). He talks about the analyst's cross, how his integrity and identity are threatened by regression and being flooded by sexuality and psychosis. The analyst could bear the cross, when the patient is "kept in sexual abstinence, in unrequited love," although this, as Freud adds, "of course is not always possible." And he concludes: "The more you let him find love the sooner you will get his complexes, but the smaller is the final success, as he gives up the fulfilments of the complexes only because he can exchange them for the results of the transference" (Meng and Freud, p. 39). Freud's conclusion is that it is absolutely *vital* to "surmount countertransference" (McGuire, 1974, p. 291), not only that, but to do so *"completely"* (Nunberg and Federn, 1962, 9.3.1910; see also Binswanger, 1956, p. 65).

On the other hand, Freud uses a well-known metaphor in describing how important the unconscious of the analyst is as "a receptive organ" capturing the messages coming from the patient—the "telephone receiver . . . adjusted to the transmitting microphone" (1912, pp. 115–116), a device that enables the doctor's unconscious "to reconstruct that unconscious, which has determined the patient's free associations" (p. 116). In *Totem and Taboo* (1913, p. 159) he postulates a transmission of "mental processes. . . . For psycho-analysis has shown us that everyone possesses in his unconscious mental activity an apparatus which enables him to . . . undo the distortions which other people have imposed on the expression of their feelings"—an idea that Ferenczi immediately describes as "new and excellent" (Brabant et al., 1992). Or, picking up Ferenczi's idea of the *Dialogues of the Unconscious* (Ferenczi, 1915, p. 109), Freud states that "the *Ucs.* of one human being can react upon that of another" (Freud, 1915, p. 194).

It seems that Freud continued to stay in what we could call a "dialectic" position: on the one side the exigency to *overcome* transference and countertransference and on the other side the fundamental *need* for transference as the basic motivation of the cure and for countertransference as the basic tool of understanding.

For Ferenczi, who had the experience of both roles—analyst and analysand—the problem was even more painful. Driven by his own conflicts, he was nevertheless able to develop a view of the therapeutic relationship that proved to be very fruitful, notwithstanding the sometimes extreme form in which he presented it. These events very probably contributed to his increasing understanding that the analyst's attitude was a *variable* in the therapeutic equation and, for that reason, he put it at the center of his interests. It was distressing for him, in fact, in the network of relationships between Freud, Elma, and himself, not to be able to distinguish *"transference"* from *"real"* feelings. He might well have found difficulty in straddling the roles of analyst, analysand, lover, friend, and follower when he threw himself wholly into those relationships. It is indeed understandable that he was able to see with great acuity how patients might sometimes suffer from what he felt was the professional "hypocrisy" (1933, pp. 158–159) of the analyst's total "abstinence"; i.e., in hiding himself behind an attitude of reserve and distance for defensive reasons and protection. Perhaps Ferenczi felt that Freud's attitude toward him during their analysis was too distant. "He was too great for me, too much of the father" he wrote to Groddeck (Dupont, 1986, pp. 36–37).

Freud, for his part, reaches a sort of conclusion: A method, repeating rather than remembering, that works with current feelings "implies conjuring up a piece of real life; and for that reason it cannot always be harmless and unobjectionable" (1914, p. 152) and since "healing through love" is something that is sought by the analysand, but which must fail in the end because of the "patient's incapacity for love" (1914, p. 101), he concludes: "In my opinion, therefore, it is *not permissible* to disavow the indifference one has developed by keeping the countertransference in check" (1915, p. 164; our translation [which we think does Freud's words more justice] and italics).

After the Budapest Congress (1918)– The Contributions of Ferenczi

After the Budapest Congress (1918), Freud seems to have preferred to leave the largely unresolved question of the practical impact of affective forces more and more to his circle, particularly Ferenczi and Rank, from whom he expected new ideas. He also offered encouragement to others in the form of a prize for the best study on the mutual influence of theory and technique (Freud, 1922). He apparently hoped that others could contribute to solving this problem. In particular he might have expected much from Ferenczi and Rank, whom he had for years encouraged to investigate questions of technique.

There is a clear connection between Freud's expectations and Ferenczi's radicalization of the concept of transference in 1926, when, following Rank, Ferenczi regarded "the relation of patient to analyst as the cardinal point of the analytic material and . . . *every* dream, *every* gesture, *every* parapraxis, *every* aggravation or improvement in the condition of the patient as above all an expression of transference and resistance" (p. 225). Today, practically the entire psychoanalytic community has taken up the central role of analyzing the transference, the importance—beyond the oedipal bond—of the mother and, to some extent, traumatism, forgetting that attention to these concerns is the historical legacy of Ferenczi, who developed these ideas during the time of his closest collaboration with Freud. The latter, incidentally, acknowledged their importance (see, for example, the circular letter in which Freud states that he values "the joint book [by Ferenczi and Rank] as a corrective of my view of the role of repetition or acting out in analysis" (Abraham and Freud, 1956, p. 345).

The topics of deep regressive states, of the repetition of trauma in the analytic interaction, of the central role of *countertransference* and, consequently, of the necessity of a *metapsychology* of the analyst, became a subject of *controversies* between Ferenczi and Freud, particularly after 1927 until Ferenczi's death in 1933. These controversies acted, as Balint reminded us, as a trauma for the analytic community, and became for long years tabooed topics, surrounded by silence, all the more in that Jones's biography on Freud had treated this subject very insufficiently. Ferenczi himself (and also Rank, his friend for some time), though not obliterated from the historical record of psychoanalysis, were viewed as being disturbed, even mentally ill (Jones, 1957, p. 47), and their theories as an outcome of this supposed mental illness.

This second, not "accepted" part of the heritage, however, was brought to London by Michael Balint, where it fell on fertile ground in the British "Middle Group" and has since, through their influence (Heimann, Little, Winnicott, and others) infiltrated current psychoanalytic thinking. Anna Freud, too, expressed her admiration for Ferenczi (see, for example, her letter to Balint of 23.5.1935 [Balint Archives, n.d.]) and borrowed one of her central terms, "developmental lines," from him. The American interpersonal school is also directly descended from Ferenczi via the mediation of Clara Thompson, who had gone to Europe for analysis with Ferenczi and subsequently analyzed Harry Stack Sullivan. In addition, as some of these issues reemerge in self psychology, we should recall that Paul Ornstein worked closely with Balint before becoming an associate of Heinz Kohut and that John Gedo, an early associate of Kohut, thoroughly studied Ferenczi.

Conclusion

From the beginning, the affective component in the psychoanalytic encounter has presented a problem. Freud first grasped the significance of these disturbances as tied to the subject's past. This view did not provide a satisfactory and definitive global solution of the difficulties, so Freud developed a twofold position, as he became gradually aware that the illusion of transference could produce a disturbance of the perception of actuality in both analyst and analysand. These interactions in the present, exchanges of feelings and their representations, became the object of further investigation and lively exchanges between Freud and his circle, especially with Ferenczi. The latter emphasized the fundamental importance of the analyst's feeling as a tool in understanding the psychoanalytic process and came to innovative ideas in understanding the patients' behavior as transference, in stressing the importance of interactions, the role of the mother, etc. These ideas were in part retained by the psychoanalytic community (very often without explicit reference to their originator), and in part rejected as a consequence of Freud's reluctance to accept them in the form they were proposed (mutual analysis; the reliving of trauma in psychoanalysis) and to an important extent also due to the resistance coming from Freud's colleagues (Abraham, Jones). With considerable latency, however, these ideas have more and more infiltrated the present psychoanalytic understanding of the therapeutic encounter.

REFERENCES

Abraham, H. & Freud, E. L., eds. (1965). *A Psycho-Analytic Dialogue: The Letters of Sigmund Freud and Karl Abraham, 1907–1926.* New York: Basic Books.

Ackerknecht, E. H. (1957). Josef Breuer über seinen Anteil an der Psychoanalyse. *Gesnerus,* 14:169–171.

Balint Archives (n.d.). Unpublished. Geneva, Switzerland: University of Geneva, Department of Psychiatry, P.O. Box 79, CH-1211/8, Geneva.

Binswanger, L. (1956). *Erinnerungen an Sigmund Freud.* Bern: Francke.

Boehlich, W., ed. (1990). *The Letters of Sigmund Freud to Eduard Silberstein, 1871–1881.* Cambridge: Harvard Univ. Press.

Brabant, E., Falzeder, E. & Giampieri-Deutsch, P., eds. (1992). *Sigmund Freud/Sándor Ferenczi, Correspondence, 1908–1914.* Paris: Calmann-Lévy.

Breuer, J. & Freud, S. (1893–1895). Studies on hysteria. *S.E.,* 2.

Decker, H. (1991). *Freud, Dora, and Vienna 1900.* New York: The Free Press.

Ferenczi, S. (1915). Psychogenetic anomalies of voice production. In: *Further Contributions to the Theory and Technique of Psycho-Analysis.* New York: Basic Books, 1955, pp. 105–109.

______ (1926). Contra-indications to the "active" psycho-analytic technique. In: *Further Contributions.* New York: Basic Books, 1955, pp. 217–230.

______ (1931). Child analysis in the analysis of adults. In: *Final Contributions.* New York: Basic Books, 1955, pp. 126–142.

______ (1932). *The Clinical Diary of Sándor Ferenczi,* ed. J. Dupont. Cambridge: Harvard Univ. Press, 1988.

______ (1933). Confusion of tongues between adults and the child. In: *Final Contributions.* New York: Basic Books, 1955, pp. 126–142.

Freud, E. & Abraham, H., eds. (1965). *A Psycho-Analytic Dialogue. The Letters of Sigmund Freud and Karl Abraham, 1907–1926.* London: Hogarth Press.

Freud, S. (1901). The psychopathology of everyday life. *S.E.,* 6 [*G.W., IV*].

______ (1905). Fragment of an analysis of a case of hysteria. *S.E.,* 7.

______ (1910). Five lectures on psycho-analysis. *S.E.,* 11.

______ (1912). Recommendations to physicians practising psycho-analysis. *S.E.,* 12.

______ (1913). Totem and taboo. *S.E.,* 13.

______ (1914a). On narcissism: An introduction. *S.E.,* 14.

_____ (1914b). Remembering, repeating and working through. *S.E.*, 12.
_____ (1915). Observations on transference love. *S.E.*, 12.
_____ (1920). Beyond the pleasure principle. *S.E.*, 18.
_____ (1922). Prize offer. *S.E.*, 17.
Hirschmüller, A. (1978). *Physiologie und Psychoanalyse in Leben und Werk Josef Breuers.* Bern: Hans Huber.
Jones, E. (1957). *Life and Work of Sigmund Freud, Vol. 3.* New York: Basic Books, 1957.
McGuire, W., ed. (1974). *The Freud-Jung Letters.* Princeton: Princeton Univ. Press.
Meng, H. & Freud, E., eds. (1963). *Psychoanalysis and Faith. The Letters of Sigmund Freud and Oskar Pfister.* New York: Basic Books.
Nunberg, H. & Federn, E., eds. (1962). *Minutes of the Vienna Psychoanalytic Society, Vol. I, 1906–1908.* New York: Int. Univ. Press.

Department of Psychiatry
P.O. Box 79
CH-1211/8 Geneva/Switzerland

Reality and Psychic Reality in Ernst Kris's Last Papers: An Attempt to Update His Findings

MARTIN S. BERGMANN

IN A WELL-KNOWN LETTER WRITTEN on September 21, 1897, Freud confided to Fliess that he no longer believed in his "neurotica." He was referring, of course, to his seduction theory. Among the reasons he cites: "there are no indications of reality in the unconscious, so that one cannot distinguish between truth and fiction that has been cathected with affect" (Masson, 1985, p. 264). Since then the distinction between "psychical reality" and "material reality," to use Freud's terms (1900, p. 620), remains central to psychoanalytic theory and technique.

In his last three papers written just a year before his death, Ernst Kris (1956a,b,c) challenged the clear-cut distinction between memories and fantasies. He outlined a major technical change by shifting his clinical emphasis away from the actual historical reality to the nature of the psychoanalytic hour itself. Kris argued that in a productive analysis every hour had its unique structure. Dreams, fantasies, memories, and current events, as well as transference reactions, were enlivened by the flow of the hour. Thus the hour had a reality of its own that was bound to affect the conceptualization of actuality and illusion. It is my contention that because Kris died prematurely—he was only 57 years old—the

Martin Bergmann is Clinical Professor of Psychology, New York University Postdoctoral Program in Psychoanalysis and Psychotherapy. He is a Training and Supervising Analyst at the New York Freudian Society.

far-reaching implications of his discoveries have not been sufficiently recognized.

To support my contention I shall first review how Freud conceived the distinction between actuality and illusions, then discuss three papers by Kris, and finally suggest the technical implications of his ideas.

Reality and Fantasy in Freud

In 1908 and again in 1911 Freud postulated that the growing child slowly, reluctantly, and incompletely relinquished wish-fulfillment fantasies in favor of reality, keeping islands of fantasy protected from the obedience to the reality principle. To the extent to which reality predominated, secondary-process thinking, obeying the laws of logic, replaced primary processes, which obeyed the pleasure principle. Neurotics, Freud emphasized, turned away from reality because they found it unbearable, either in whole or in part.

In the introductory lectures Freud addressed his vexing problem of reality and fantasy as they mold childhood memories. "Scenes from infancy are not always true. Indeed, they are not true in the majority of cases, and in a few of them they are the direct opposite of the historical truth" (1916–1917, p. 367). Were they always true or always false the work of the psychoanalyst would be easier, but Freud made it clear that memories are frequently compounds of truth and falsehood. "The fantasies possess *psychical* as contrasted with *material* reality, and we gradually learn to understand that *in the world of neurosis it is psychical reality which is the decisive kind*" (p. 368).

Freud enumerated particular subjects wherein fantasy and reality were particularly difficult to disentangle: observation of parental intercourse, seduction by an adult, and a threat of being castrated. To account for the central role these play in every analysis, Freud called these primal fantasies. These "were once real occurrences in the primaeval times of the human family, and . . . children in their phantasies are simply filling in the gaps in individual truth with prehistoric truth" (p. 371).

In the paper entitled *A Case of Homosexuality in a Woman* (1920), Freud stated,

> So long as we trace the development from its final outcome backwards, the chain of events appears continuous, and we feel we have gained an insight which is completely satisfactory or even exhaustive. But if we proceed in the reverse way, if we start from the premises inferred from the analysis and try to follow these up to the final results, then we no longer get the impression of an inevitable sequence of events which could not have been otherwise determined [p. 167].

This was a significant statement on Freud's part. It is the unique interaction between fantasy and reality that cannot be predicted. We can only try to make sense of what happened. The analyst cannot predict, but he can reconstruct for the analysand what the latter fails to remember.

How important is it that the analyst's reconstruction be historically accurate? In his 1937 paper Freud was simultaneously tolerant and defensive: "no damage is done if, for once in a way, we make a mistake and offer the patient a wrong construction as the probable historical truth. . . . What in fact occurs in such an event is rather that the patient remains as though he were untouched by what has been said and reacts to it with neither a 'Yes' nor a 'No'. . . . I can assert without boasting that such an abuse of 'suggestion' has never occurred in my practice" (pp. 261–262).

With the advent of ego psychology these views became untenable. Although the id may not recognize a discernible difference between reality and fantasy, to the ego it matters greatly whether the child fantasizes the seduction or primal scene or encountered it in reality. When the child fantasizes it is because he is ready to elaborate these fantasies; when he actually encounters seduction he is not ready for it, and indeed cannot be ready. Such a real event inevitably affects the child's object relations, often destroying trust; fantasy alone has a far less devastating effect. Today skilled psychoanalysts can and must attempt to distinguish between the two, as I hope to show in my discussion.

After Freud laid the foundation for psychoanalytic ego psychology in 1926, Waelder (1937) in the context of the debate over Melanie Klein's ideas, further clarified the distinction between fantasy and reality. Unlike the Viennese who elaborated upon Freud's new ideas about the ego, Klein pursued a line of thought that branched off from Freud's (1920) formulation of the dual instinct theory. She was influenced by the ideas of Ferenczi and Abraham on symbolism and emphasized the oral phase. She postulated that the first year of the infant's life was one of high anxiety and inner terror, dominated by the projection and introjection of aggression belonging to the death instinct. She hypothesized that as the result of the projection of his aggressive wishes the infant felt endangered by a supposedly malevolent person or part object (Riviere, 1936). These projected fantasies are, psychologically speaking, not fantasies at all, since they are perceived by the infant as real. Waelder interpreted Klein's work to mean that the reality of the infant's treatment by his caretakers confirmed or refuted these anxieties but remained secondary to the early fantasies.

Waelder countered with an account of the genesis of fantasies in young children and their relation to material reality. In his view children's fantasies did not originate in a basic fantasy and/or arise from a need to project overwhelming and threatening aggression derived from the death instinct. Rather they originated in some event in the child's actual life such as the mother's pregnancy, the arrival of a sibling, organic illness, or separation from the mother, which the child interpreted in his own way. One could never understand a child's fantasies without reference to the child's reality, he argued.

The controversy about the role of fantasy between ego psychologists and the Kleinians went back to the role Freud assigned to "primal fantasies." Klein took as her starting point the idea that every child, regardless of his history, used fantasy in order to cope with the overwhelming aggressive wishes present from birth. These fantasies found symbolic expression in play and dreams; and since these primal fantasies were always searching to emerge in symbolic form, Klein thought it legitimate to interpret them as soon as possible (Klein, 1943).

The Reconceptualization of Ernst Kris

An essential member of the Hartmann circle of ego psychologists, Kris shared their conviction that confirmation and disconfirmation of psychoanalytic hypotheses will come from direct child observation and that it was time for psychoanalysis to become a general psychology. This meant that psychoanalysis needed to be extended through further study of what they had articulated as the conflict-free sphere of the ego (Bergmann, 1993). This conviction led them to a new emphasis on the ego's ability to neutralize derivatives of the aggressive as well as the sexual drive. Kris's first paper addressing memory dealt with a new term he coined: the personal myth.

The Personal Myth

The Personal Myth: A Problem in Psychoanalytic Technique (1956a) described a group of patients whose personal history was more than an essential part of their self-representation. It was a treasured possession to which they clung. Unless the therapist was alerted to its presence, Kris argued, such a personal myth was often strong enough to survive psychoanalysis intact. The personal myth falsified the self-representations and replaced them with wishful self-representations. The term was akin, but not identical, to Winnicott's (1960) "false self."

The personal myth was not repressed, but it helped repress painful childhood memories not in keeping with it. Separate details that compose the myth were conscious, but the analysand did not realize how they had been woven into the fabric of his conscious autobiography. To recognize the myth's existence, its influence, and the damage it caused was a painful part of the working-through process. The analyst who uncovered the personal myth ferreted out falsification of memories, lacunae in the continuity of biography, and other distortions. One of the myth's damaging effects was that it compelled patients to actions that fulfilled its demands. The myth served many purposes, including idealization of parents, concretizing family-romance fantasies, denying early traumatic events, and screening early depressive or anxiety states.

In one of the cases Kris presented the personal myth eliminated the relationship between the patient and her mother and substituted a fantasy of a beloved nurse the patient had lost in early childhood. Kris, in keeping with then-current ego psychology, stressed mainly the defensive function of the personal myth. Clearly, such a myth also has a comforting function, acting as a substitute for a love object and masking the grave limitations of the real parent.

One of my analysands, who lost her father during her first year of life, created a belief that she alone was loyal to his memory and therefore had a special relationship with him. Instead of developing the usual oedipal wishes with her stepfather, she remained attached to the fantasy of her dead father, who now belonged entirely to her. While mother and siblings accepted the stepfather as their father, my patient remained aloof from him. This attachment to the dead father contributed to a state of permanent mourning for him, giving the personality of the patient a persistent depressive cast.

The Recovery of Childhood Memory

Kris's next paper (1956b) expanded on ideas in the previous one. He suggested that personal memory was the least autonomous area of memory functioning. It telescoped events and libidinized memories. As a result, reconstructive work often miscarried, and a sheltering fantasy survived the analysis.

Following Anna Freud's (1951) lead, Kris noted the surprising fact that a stress trauma covering many years usually appeared in memory as a single event. Conversely, traumatic events like seduction at an early age did not appear in sharp outline. In Kris's view the line of demarcation between memories and screen memories was fluid. No memories were mere records of past events. The present always exerted pressure on what would be called and what would be repressed. The need for meaning played havoc with actual childhood events, creating new combinations and recombinations.

Kris cited a child, Dorothy, in her third year of life (p. 325). Her younger brother had been born when she was two. The relationship between her parents had been and continued to be stormy; a beloved dog had chewed the tail of her cat; a few months later this dog had been run over and killed; her grandfather had died. Kris questioned the probability that future analysts would be able to recover these events discretely separated from each other.

Dorothy's next few years brought other events that taxed her ego's capacity to integrate them. Kris concluded that the number of events requiring integration was almost infinite. The task of reconstructing these events was beyond the capacity of any analyst. All occurrences were subject to the selective scrutiny of memory, but as such processes were repeated they achieved a meaning and became integrated into the structure of the personality. With this understanding Kris reached a significant new insight. The events were molded into patterns, he argued, and a psychoanalysis dealt not directly with events but with the patterns into which these events have been arranged by the selective scrutiny of memory. Dorothy's ego would have the task of putting all these events into a coherent structure or a coherent story that would make sense to the child in her third year of life and subsequently. He asked, would she be able to assimilate the events or would they overtax the integrative function of her young ego, forcing her to develop a personal myth?

The Vicissitudes of Insight in the Course of Psychoanalysis

In this paper (1956c) Kris applied to the analytic hour an idea that he first developed in 1935 in his studies on art. He differentiated two types of regression. In the first the ego is overwhelmed by regression resulting in pathology. In the second the regression takes place under the control of the ego. Only artists and other creative people were thought to be capable of such creative regression. Kris now applied the concept to the analytic hour itself. This paper is related to the two previous ones by showing the optimal conditions under which childhood memories or fantasies emerge. In the good hour the analysand is not straining to find new memories; they appeared unbidden. The capacity to uncover new memories coincided with the capacity to grasp the significance of what had been uncovered. In the "good hour" memories appear in context, symbolizing significant events or a reorientation of the psychic structure in the life of the patient.

Although psychoanalysts had long known that certain analytic hours were regarded by both patient and analyst as particularly productive, Kris was the first to examine such an hour systematically. He described such hours as generally beginning with the patient recounting a recent experience. The analysand was restless, he then expressed negative feelings toward the analyst. But at a certain point in the hour a marked change occurred. Everything seemed to fall into place. A dream was told, and there was no resistance to associating to it. New memories became available. Often all that the analyst needed to do was ask one or two questions and the analysand summed up by himself or herself.

Kris differentiated the "good hour" from the deceptively good hour, the difference being due to the transference. In the deceptively good hour the patient wished to obtain the analyst's love and so produced associations the analyst would appreciate. The same thing happened when the transference was fueled by either strong merger wishes or by competitive wishes. In the deceptively good hour the analysand is making his own interpretations because he wishes either to be merged with the analyst or to be ahead of him. When the free-association process was not autonomous a genuine good hour would not emerge. In keeping with the vocabulary of the Hartmann period of ego psychology, Kris stressed the neutralization of aggression that takes place early in the hour, brought about by the verbalization of the negative transference. The expression of the negative transference enabled the integrative function of the ego to become freer and directed the process of association. This process was under the influence of autonomous functions of the ego, which in turn made insight possible.

Since only a few analysts today operate with the concept of autonomous functions, we have to question anew why the expression of negative transference is so crucial to the emergence of the good hour? In retrospect we can see that the negative affect is due to a preexisting equilibrium being called into question. The conflict between the wish to uphold the compromise formation and the wish to be liberated from its oppression is responsible for the negative affect. This much is clear: when aggressive feelings generated during analysis find no outlet, the integrative function of patients cannot operate freely.

One of the implications of Kris's concept of the good hour is that it is the analysand's property and cannot be willed either by analyst or analysand. However, an analyst can act as midwife to the good hour, or, conversely, help prevent its emergence. Only rarely should the analyst introduce into an hour material not brought in by the patient. Among an analyst's technical errors that can interfere with the good hour are interventions early in the hour and questions or interpretations that deflect the association's flow into channels that occupy the analyst or seem urgent to him rather than following the analysand's associations and allowing the hour to unfold. Another interference can occur when the analysand reaches a block, cannot find his way out, and the analyst leaves him to struggle by himself. Feeling deserted, the analysand gives up the search. When the analysis is blocked, the analyst should direct his attention solely to the nature of the block. The analyst should not interfere and try to interpret ahead of the analysand when the latter is working by himself.

In different ways Kris's three papers focused on the role of the integrative functions of the ego. At times the mere asking for a connection between different topics within one hour stimulates the integrative function of the analysand's ego. Or, to give another technical example, when the associations to a dream fail to make intelligible the transition from the manifest content to the latent content, the analyst can invite the patient to simply enumerate the various themes present in the dream and the associations. The mere invitation is often enough to stimulate the integrative function. Alternatively, the analyst may examine the free associations to a dream to discover why they failed to achieve what they intended. He will then notice that the free associations were not as productive as they could have been because they took place under the dominance of the superego or because anxiety or depression interfered. When the analyst draws the attention of the analysand to such circumstances more productive associations will often emerge.

Unlike the division of labor that prevailed in classical analysis the analysand, after Kris, was no longer confined to the production of free association and the analyst was no longer the only one endowed by virtue of his professional training with the capacity to tell the patient what the free associations meant. In spite of the fact that during the process of free associations the ego is asked to abstain from criticism and give up its role as censor of the id, the capacity to free associate is itself a complex ego function. But after Kris, it is not the only ego function that needs to be cultivated. The integrative functions of the ego also must be developed, so the analysand can find the connection that converts free associations into insight. The analytic process therefore activates two different ego functions that must work in harmony with each other.

Discussion

For Freud reconstruction became necessary whenever childhood memories failed to appear. Reconstructions were shortcuts when the analyst could not discover why the memories he was looking for failed to emerge. For Kris, since the appearance of memories was no longer crucial to the psychoanalytic enterprise, reconstructions did not aim to recapture an event in the literal sense but claimed to recapture a class of events that could account for a puzzling piece of behavior. The analyst's main task became to guard the analytic process and at times set it in motion. This did not imply passivity for the analyst; without his interventions most patients' associations would be repetitive and circuitous. Once the process has begun the analyst safeguards it by interpretation that demonstrates to the analysand unsuspected connections that his own integrative functions are not yet capable of reaching. Increasingly in the course of a good analysis the analysand not only free associates but also attempts to make his own interpretations, including reconstructions.

To the question of reality and illusion in the analytic encounter Kris made a unique contribution. When he coined the term "personal myth" and pointed out its dangers in terms of reality testing and the danger of fictional self-representations, he called attention to the need for psychoanalysis to include the contribution of the fictional personal myth. On the other hand, Kris did not believe that the past as it was lived could ever be recaptured in adult memory: analysands revealed not events but patterns.

While putting himself in opposition to many analysts who still believed that events as they happened could be faithfully recaptured, Kris nevertheless insisted on analyzing fantasies about the personal myth. He introduced into psychoanalysis a degree of sophistication that went beyond the simple reality-fantasy division and has yet to be fully assimilated. The analysand's willingness to tell all and his capacity to free associate have always been the prerequisites for a successful analysis (A. Kris, 1982). The difficulty so many analysands have in acquiring the capacity to free associate constitutes an important chapter in psychoanalytic technique (Bergmann & Hartmann, 1976). We owe to Kris the insight that the integrative functions of the ego are just as important in a successful analysis as the capacity to free associate. When the analysand has acquired the capacity to do both, the complex web in which actuality and illusion are intertwined, although never fully resolved, will cease to be a burden to the future analysand.

Kris accomplished more than he realized. When he shifted the emphasis from the content of the past to the structure of the hour he shifted the analyst's attention to process. There was no need for the analyst to decide whether a seduction took place or whether it was imagined. Following Kris, the decision between fantasy and reality needed to be left to the integrative function of the analysand's ego. But clinical experience has taught us that the analyst plays a part in that decision by attending to defensive processes and interpreting resistances. We know from experience that when patients are dealing with seduction wishes they tend to favor the seduction theory as a defense. Conversely, if seduction has actually occurred, the patient will frequently make every effort to defend the seducing adult and accuse himself or herself of fantasizing or being crazy. Such a myth impedes the integrative function of the ego and requires the analyst's intervention. When the analyst is successful in discovering the resistance that inhibits the two basic ego functions, free association and the integrative capacity, and translates it into insight, his work is essentially done and the patient is ready to exchange analysis for self-analysis.

REFERENCES

Bergmann, M. S. (1993). Reflections on the history of psychoanalysis. (Plenary address at the American Psychoanalytic Association.) *J. Amer. Psychoanal. Assn.*, 41:4.

_____ & Hartmann, F. R. (1976). *The Evolution of Psychoanalytic Technique.* New York: Columbia Univ. Press.

Freud, A. (1951). Observations on child development. *Writings of Anna Freud, Vol. 4,* pp. 143–162. New York: Int. Univ. Press.

Freud, S. (1900). The interpretation of dreams. *S.E.,* 5.

_____ (1908). Creative writers and daydreaming. *S.E.,* 9.

_____ (1911). Formulations on two principles of mental functioning. *S.E.,* 12.

_____ (1916–1917). Introductory lectures on psycho-analysis (Part III). *S.E.,* 16.

_____ (1920). The psychogenesis of a case of homosexuality in a woman. *S.E.,* 18.

_____ (1937). Constructions in analysis. *S.E.,* 23.

Klein, M. (1943). Memorandum on her technique. In: *The Freud-Klein Controversies: 1941 to 1945,* ed. P. King & R. Steiner. London: Tavistock-Routledge, 1991, pp. 635–638.

Kris, A. O. (1982). *Free Association Methods and Process.* New Haven, CT: Yale Univ. Press.

Kris, E. (1935). The psychology of caricature. In: *Psychoanalytic Exploration in Art.* New York: Int. Univ. Press, 1952, pp. 173–188.

_____ (1956a). The personal myth: A problem in psychoanalytic technique. In: *The Selected Papers of Ernst Kris.* New Haven, CT: Yale Univ. Press, 1975, pp. 272–300.

_____ (1956b). The recovery of childhood memories in psychoanalysis. In: *The Selected Papers of Ernst Kris.* New Haven, CT: Yale Univ. Press, 1975, pp. 301–340.

_____ (1956c). On some vicissitudes of insight in psychoanalysis. In: *The Selected Papers of Ernst Kris.* New Haven, CT: Yale Univ. Press, 1975, pp. 252–271.

Masson, J. M., ed. (1985). *The Complete Letters of Sigmund Freud to Wilhelm Fliess: 1887–1904.* Cambridge: Harvard Univ. Press.

Riviere, J. (1936). On the genesis of psychical conflict in earliest infancy. *Internat. J. Psycho-Anal.,* 17:395–422.

Waelder, R. (1937). The problem of the genesis of psychical conflict in earliest infancy. *Internat. J. Psycho-Anal.,* 18:406–473.

Winnicott, D. W. (1960). Ego distortions in terms of true and false self. In: *The Maturational Process and the Facilitating Environment.* New York: Int. Univ. Press, 1965, pp. 140–152.

1136 Fifth Avenue
New York, NY 10128

Actuality and Illusion in the Transference: A Brief Discussion

HOWARD B. LEVINE, M.D.

IS THERE—OR SHOULD THERE BE DRAWN—a meaningful distinction between actuality and illusion in psychoanalytic theory and practice? At first glance, such a question may seem trivial. Our everyday common sense helps us to distinguish truth from distortion, reality from fantasy. However, as the various contributions to this issue have demonstrated, "truth" and "reality" in psychoanalysis are neither everyday nor common-sensical. The monumental discovery that led Freud to renounce his seduction theory was not the Oedipus complex per se, but rather his recognition of a realm of complex mental functioning in which unconscious fantasies join with historical events as major organizational determinants in the construction of individual experience, a realm he called "psychic reality."

While enriching the scope and complexity of psychoanalytic theory, Freud's elevation of the concept of psychic reality to a central place in his theory introduced an epistemological dilemma with which current analytic theorists, including many of our contributors, continue to struggle. As noted in our introduction, "the separation of actuality and illusion is not as clearcut and straightforward as had been assumed." Our once-held supposition that within the analytic relationship, distinctions such as internal and external, subject and object, observer and observed are

Dr. Levine is a member of the faculty at the Boston Psychoanalytic Institute and at the Massachusetts Institute for Psychoanalysis.

absolute and inviolable has been replaced by an appreciation of the ever-shifting dialectical relationship that exists between these categories of experience.

During his formative years, Freud was deeply immersed in and committed to the scientific rationalism of Helmholtz (Jones, 1961). In his later life, residues of this philosophy continued to inhere in his thinking, as, for example, in his metaphor of the analyst as archaeologist, patiently digging in the depths of the unconscious for the shards of the buried (veridical) past (Freud, 1937) or his belief that a distinction could be drawn between the reality of the social realm, in which the rules of ordinary etiquette and manners held sway, and the illusion impregnated realm of the consulting room, in which the rules of proper analytic technique were to obtain. As noted by Hoffer, it was this latter distinction that allowed Freud to attempt to analyze his own daughter, Anna, even as they lived together and shared the common life of their domestic relations or to propose to Ferenczi that he join the Freud family for a shared summer vacation, which would include two hours of analysis per day.

That Freud was also wary of such arrangements, at least in the case of Ferenczi, whom he feared might be alienated and lost to him and the psychoanalytic movement should a negative transference arise and become unmanagable, is also clear. As described by Haynal and Falzeder, Freud's own clinical experiences, as well as those of Breuer, Jung, and Ferenczi, more than alerted him to the actual dangers inherent in the analyst's subjectivity, especially the potential for the analyst to respond to the transference affects of his/her patients with unconscious, conflict-derived and motivated affects and actions of his/her own.

But our current struggles with truth and illusion in psychoanalysis go far beyond the position that it is only the unresolved neurosis and conflicts of the analyst or the analyst's affective response to the patient's transference (i.e., the countertransference in its narrowest sense) that is the source of difficulty. For along with Freud the archaeologist (or positivist), there was also a Freud who was essentially an hermeneuticist (or phenomenologist). And this latter trend in Freud's thinking even predated his renunciation of the seduction theory.

At least as early as his paper on Screen Memories, Freud (1899) was aware that the patient's memory was an inconstant ally in the treatment process; that there was little hope of obtaining a connected life narrative from a patient that would reach back beyond the age of six or seven; or that what was most important in the past would be what the neurotic patient remembered. "The experiences of the earliest years of our childhood leave ineradicable traces in the depths of our minds. If, however, we seek in our memories . . . the impressions that were destined to influence us to the end of our lives" we are bound to be disappointed (p. 303). In fact, his finding that neurotics forgot essential pathogenic components of events, while remembering inessential incidental components of those same events was, at that time, almost an intrinsic part of Freud's operational definition, or at least his *description,* of neurotic psychopathology.

The problem, of course, was that of the unconscious. By definition, the latter is not directly observable but can only be intuited by the effects that it has on one's thoughts and actions. The situation was much like Plato's cave, in which the essences of things can never be directly noted but can only be inferred by the reflected appearance of their shadows.

Freud's conclusions in this early paper are particularly striking in the light of our current views of memory, perception, the nature of experience, and the data of therapy and are quite relevant to the matter of actuality and illusion:

> It may indeed be questioned whether we have any memories at all *from* our childhood: memories *relating to* our childhood may be all that we possess. Our childhood memories show us our earliest years not as they were but as they appeared at the later periods when the memories were aroused. In these periods of arousal, the childhood memories did not, as people are accustomed to say, *emerge;* they were *formed* at that time. And a number of motives, with no concern for historical accuracy had a part in forming them, as well as in the selection of the memories themselves [p. 322].

The motives Freud discussed in the Screen Memories paper were those of defense and representation. To these, we would now add—and emphasize—the object relational context (especially the transference) in which the memory is produced.

A careful delineation of the lifelong, internal, theoretical struggle that was waged within Freud between the positivist/archaeologist and the phenomenologist/hermeneuticist would take us far beyond the confines of the space allotted to this discussion. Some of its outlines have already been alluded to by Haynal and Falzeder as they trace Freud's attempts to conceptualize the problem of the analyst's affects in the analysis. Suffice to say, from Freud onward, actuality and illusion have appeared in psychoanalytic discussions as markers of this recurring epistemological dilemma, sometimes as if they were antagonists, sometimes as if parts of a dialectical whole.

From this perspective, Bergmann's paper is striking, because it shows one thrust of the work of Ernst Kris, that consummate ego psychologist—ego psychology with its connotations of the rational and objective conceptually separated and preserved from the malestrom of the irrational by the concepts of relative autonomy and the conflict-free sphere—to be squarely in the camp of the hermeneuticists. That is, if memory is as mutable as Freud and Kris have asserted it to be, and if, as Bergmann notes, Kris has taught us that the words of our analysands do not only reveal past events, but also *the patterns of organization* that are in part the consequences of those events and that underlie and structure the patient's mental functioning, then historical (veridical) truth in the analytic context often becomes secondary to the more "immediate," highly context-specific truth (psychic reality) that emerges or is jointly created in the analytic relationship.

Contemporary clinical theorists—McLaughlin (1981, 1991), Hoffman (1983), Atwood and Stolorow (1984), Loewald (1986), Gill (1988, 1990), Boesky (1990), Modell (1990), Jacobs (1991), Poland (1992), to name just a few—have increasingly tried to take account of the interactional and/or intersubjective dimensions of the analytic relationship, without abandoning depth psychology for a simplistic interactionism. In such views, considerations of actuality and illusion are inextricably tied to conceptualizations of the analytic situation as a dyadic, intersubjective experience. Seen from this perspective, the issue may become less one of reality versus fantasy, actuality versus illusion, and more that of, "Whose reality is it?" Or, as F. Levine and Hoffer have each implied, "To what purposes will either participant's 'reality' be put within the analysis?" Their contributions challenge us to examine where a given clinician or theorist judges the appropriate analytic surface to lie and to ask, "What is the relevant analytic datum, to which party in the analytic dyad does it belong, and to what extent can it be construed as belonging to either member of the analytic dyad?"

It is interesting to note that each of our clinical papers—Feldman, First, and Skolnikoff have, in different ways, attempted to elaborate upon the interactional, intersubjective dimensions of the analysis. Here, the concepts of enactment, countertransference—in the broad sense of the totality of the analyst's emotional response to the patient and the analysis—and "projective identification" seem to furnish a series of nodal points for further dialogue and discussion.

As I read them, each of these clinical contributors shares the expectation that the relevant analytic data, that which reflects the most useful analytic surface and is the product of the most immediate, transferentially determined psychic reality, will emerge as something alive within the moment between a given analytic pair. This "something" is often jointly enacted—or at least experienced by both members of the analytic dyad as a pressure toward some concrete interaction or mode of relationship. Skolnikoff may emphasize the inevitability of the analyst's countertransference enactments—and even implies that the identificatory processes that drive them are essential elements of a successful analytic engagement; First may emphasize the importance and use of the countertransference in Winnicott's sense of actually providing a good-enough holding environment within the analytic relationship; and Feldman may speak in terms of projective identification, but as is reflected in their clinical material, the technique of each author is deeply grounded in the here-and-now manifestations of the transference as they are jointly constructed, experienced, and lived out within the analytic relationship. For each of these contributors, the patient's experience of the transference is not just experienced and reported in the words of the patient. Rather, it is actively, inevitably, and unconsciously created in the analytic process by both analyst and analysand. This view that the form of the transference is a product of the analytic interaction rather than the sole responsibility of the patient's unconscious is a position of which both the contemporary Kleinians (e.g., Spillius [1988] and Gill [1988, 1990]) would doubtless approve.

Perhaps the most divergent views among our contributors regarding the actuality/illusion controversy are offered by F. Levine and Olinick. For the former, the "real relationship" that exists between analyst and analysand is always, at least in part, a figment of one or the other's imagination, constructed for purposes of unconscious defense and/or gratification. For the latter, the literal and concrete, actual structural attributes of the transference are such that they will inevitably work toward interfering with the analyst's capacity to understand, and therefore meaningfully interpret, the patient's transference experience and the uses to which it is being put.

Given the complexity of the subject and the variety of our authors' responses, it is clear that the many issues which have been raised are far from settled. Rather than some definitive "solution" to the problems of actuality and illusion in the analytic encounter, it must suffice to note that previous views of a potentially winnable struggle between polar opposites—objective vs. subjective, actuality vs. illusion—have for the most part quietly given way to an appreciation of a dialectical complexity that continues to evolve within the intersubjective matrix of the analytic process.

For analyst as well as patient, the experience of the analysis is inexorably subjective. From a pragmatic point of view, then, the question of whether something is actual or illusory may be moot. Analyst and patient alike can only know and use what they feel. Subjectivity of experience is all that either party may possess. And while we may be discomfitted by this realization that we will never fully know *the* truth of our patients' lives, there is solace in recognizing that through our attempts to understand and articulate the experiences that arise from the radical subjectivity of the psychoanalytic process, objective change can occur.

REFERENCES

Atwood, G. & Stolorow, R. (1984). *Structures of Subjectivity*. Hillsdale, NJ: The Analytic Press.

Boesky, D. (1990). The psychoanalytic process and its components. *Psychoanal. Quart.*, 59:550–584.
Freud, S. (1899). Screen memories. *S.E.*, 3.
——— (1937). Constructions in analysis. *S.E.*, 23.
Gill, M. (1988). The interpersonal paradigm and the degree of the therapist's involvement. In: *Essential Papers on Countertransference*, ed. B. Wolstein. New York: New York Univ. Press, 1988, pp. 304–338.
——— (1990). Indirect suggestion: A response to Oremland's *Interpretation and Interaction*. In: Oremland, J. D. (1990), *Interpretation and Interaction*. Hillsdale, NJ: The Analytic Press, pp. 137–164.
Hoffman, I. (1983). The patient as interpreter of the analyst's experience. *Contemp. Psychoanal.*, 19:389–421.
Jacobs, T. J. (1991). *The Use of the Self.* Madison, CT: Int. Univ. Press.
Jones, E. (1961). *The Life and Work of Sigmund Freud* (abridged). New York: Basic Books.
Loewald, H. (1986). Transference-countertransference. *J. Amer. Psychoanal. Assn.*, 34:275–288.
McLaughlin, J. T. (1981). Transference, psychic reality, and countertransference. *Psychoanal. Quart.*, 50:639–664.
——— (1991). Clinical and theoretical aspects of enactment. *J. Amer. Psychoanal. Assn.*, 39:595–614.
Modell, A. (1990). *Other Times, Other Realities.* Cambridge: Harvard Univ. Press.
Poland, W. (1992). From analytic surface to analytic space. *J. Amer. Psychoanal. Assn.*, 40:381–404.
Spillius, E., ed. (1988). *Melanie Klein Today.* London: Routledge.

124 Dean Road
Brookline, MA 02146

Epilogue: Actuality, Illusion, and Clinical Authority

PROBABLY NO CLINICAL SITUATION BRINGS questions of actuality and illusion into clearer focus than the white heat of a transference neurosis and the common though much less talked about reciprocal "countertransference neurosis," which both impedes the former's resolution and is often the material out of which the transference iatrogenically fashions itself. Skolnikoff writes aptly that intersubjectivity and more than transitory identification of analyst with patient is an often unacknowledged aspect of psychoanalytic processes. Yet even in the throes of such turmoil, all clinicians operate with the necessity that the patient hear some of the analyst's words, some of the time, as illuminating his or her transference illusion, rather than as only belonging to it, and that the analyst conduct himself to make this a possibility for the patient.

All our contributors comment on an aspect of providing this necessity. To see their commentaries in context, let us consider some clinical material, selected precisely because it demonstrates a low-grade but significant countertransference interference that, at the time of the sessions presented, had not been recognized by the analyst who later reported it to me. This interference reflects the powerful way in which the analytic process has been deeply engaged by both analyst and analysand and illustrates the inevitable, reciprocal, and reverberating effects of transference and countertransference forces on the unfolding process. Although this material may not represent an instance of *ideal* technique—itself probably an illusion—it represents a common enough *actual* situation in an analysis, through which each member of the analytic pair must find some way to negotiate, if analytic progress is to be made.

Two weeks before a summer interruption, the patient began a Friday session by offering to write out the check for the bill. She thought that she remembered the amount, but nonetheless asked for verification. (She had not immediately been able to pay the bill and had mentioned frequently that she hoped the short delay would not inconvenience the analyst. The analyst reported that the patient's transference wish not to pay because she felt frustrated and withheld from for not being given a baby had been uncovered and elaborated in the work of the previous week.) This was followed by the patient's remarking that she was "hopelessly confused" by some scheduling changes.

The patient continued by noting that she had almost not recognized the analyst. He'd gotten a haircut that would last him till the end of the summer, no, until January. She then mentioned needing to take driving directions from her office for a weekend engagement. An older cousin who lived in the same area had telephoned the previous evening to announce the recent birth of two new grandchildren. The patient reported that she felt envious and that she could not listen to the detailed description of how well the infants were doing without remembering a self-righteous and wounding remark made years ago to her by the same caller about the patient's anxious deportment when her child was sick. She thought then of all the work she had to do and realized that by finishing one project she could "kill two birds with one stone." She turned next to her feelings that the analyst frustrated her by not telling her what was going on. She realized from recent work that she craved penetrating interpretations from him that would give her a baby as she had wished one from her father, but she felt that during the whole previous session he had ignored her confusion about the meaning of her associations, said nothing, and, after she got upset, spoke to her instead about her experience of him as incompetent like her mother. She had not felt he was incompetent; she realized instead she felt frustrated by him as she had by her father, but the session was over. He was withholding from her, telling himself that analysts were supposed not to talk, staying at arm's length by making comments that sounded academic and did not touch her. In doing so, he was not giving her the insight she needed to get better. She imagined what it would be like to be in treatment with an analyst who would interpret what she was talking about when she felt confused. Or would help her understand why she was confused. She would feel relieved, she would know what was going on. She would also feel that she'd been given something, that she didn't have to do all the work herself. What would happen then? She would have to recognize that it was about being given a baby and feel embarrassed and have to deal with not having gotten these things in the past. That would be painful and sad. But at least she'd know what she was talking about. This was painful too, but it was not helpful, to feel so frustrated and denied. Her thoughts went to a colleague's former husband, a self-destructive, withholding man. She described in detail his history and their contacts, then said "Why am I talking about this now?" The analyst responded, "What comes to mind?"

The patient became furious. She had been talking since the beginning of the hour. Surely that was what was coming to mind. It had to mean something, but she didn't know what. She couldn't remember all she'd said. The analyst remarked that she was feeling frustrated. The patient became more irate. Obviously she was feeling frustrated. The analyst was exacerbating her frustration by not helping her, then remarking on the feelings he made acute by asking her what came to mind when she needed more help.

The analyst responded, "If that's the case, what about your saying you envied your cousin her two new grandchildren, then talking about your own projects, then saying you could kill two birds with one stone?" The patient exploded: "So you knew all the time what I was talking about! I didn't. Why didn't you say that before? Why withhold and ask me what comes to mind when you already knew and I didn't? I'm too angry to work now. How would you expect me to feel?" She continued that she felt so enraged she was ready to walk out. She refused to talk about feelings that he accentuated by sitting there not helping her when she needed help. That wasn't what she came to analysis for. Now she was too angry to go back to her envy of her cousin and killing two birds with one stone. She paused. For that matter, she remembered, right after talking about killing two birds she'd talked about feeling frustrated by the analyst and her colleague's father dying. While continuing to attack the analyst for unnecessarily withholding and making her too angry to work, the patient began, in the short time left, to connect her feelings toward the analyst and her previous associations with various aspects of her childhood rage at her father for giving her mother babies and not giving them to her, and guilty fantasies of having killed babies in revenge.

In the material just cited, about which, for the sake of discussion, I shall accept the report that the underlying wish was indeed that of a baby from the father, the affective components of the patient's oedipal disappointment made use of the analyst's request for more associations to display themselves with full infantile force. That does not mean, however, that the patient's characterization of the analyst's intervention is invalid. There are *at least* two actualities, the patient's active, organizing unconscious fantasy/memory constellation, which directed the sequence and derivatives in her associations, her frequently professed confusions, and the force of her reaction to the analyst's intervention, and also the impact of the analyst's countertransferentially motivated intervention, which sadistically exacerbated the patient's frustration and impeded psychoanalytic work.

The interaction exemplifies a version of the clinical predicament, potentially ever present, that stems from the analyst's position as both partaking in the patient's psychic reality and, by definition, having a responsibility to comment upon it so as to make a contribution to the patient's acquisition of self-understanding. The analyst aims, in Feldman's words, for a sense of truth which comes from a convergence between the experience of the patient and analyst in relation to transference phenomena. When the analyst's words fall short, either because the patient's transference experience overwhelms his or her awareness of the illusory component, or because the analyst's mistake has derailed the patient's aim of self-inquiry, or both, how illusion is once again discerned and convergence restored becomes crucial. Elsa First offers us an account of the skillful and tactful establishment of the analyst's credibility with a patient initially too traumatized to recognize the possibility that his reactions to the analyst were influenced by his transference fantasies. The patient just described asked for help in understanding. Like all analytic actions, the request was a compromise, in this case, for argument's sake, expressing both an originally childhood, id-driven oedipal wish, and an ego-motivated adaptive need for help with a block. The analyst chose only to ask for further associations, a technical maneuver that the patient experienced as a rejection. The patient then retaliated for the felt attack by making the analyst's refusal to interpret her only subject. Partly because of his enactment, the analyst's interpretive authority was temporarily impaired.

Hoffer distinguishes the reality of the patient's passions from the use to which analysis puts them. Transference passions need to be manageable enough to leave the analyst's authority minimally intact, however. In articulating what *her* patient felt, First acted differently from her patient's expectation of his transference object, creating a space for analytic work between the actual interchange and his unconsciously influenced perception. We can hypothesize that the analyst's request for associations in the material above too closely duplicated a set of fantasies and memories involving a sadistic and disappointing primary object. Once the possibility of the patient's perceiving the difference between actuality and transference experience is restored, however, the patient can be helped to discover the function of her retaliation (to ward off the humiliation of having to ask and not having been given to), the significance of her retaliation (an attack on the analyst's authority and potency), and what she was probably retaliating for (for argument's sake, the refusal to grant her wish for a baby). In explicitly connecting enactments with wishes on both sides to undo inherent inequalities of the analytic situation, moreover, Hoffer also encourages us to consider the meaning to the patient of the analyst's apparently restorative intervention ("if that's the case . . ."), a subtle acknowledgment of the validity of the patient's criticisms and admission of error.

On the issue of the possible impact of the analyst's actions, Haynal and Falzeder remind us of the difference between Freud's and Ferenczi's reaction to the discovery of the intensity of the analyst's response to the patient's transference. Freud advised an attitude of scientific detachment, surely useful in many ways, including preventing deleterious action. It was Ferenczi, however, who recognized that even benign remoteness, to say nothing of sadistic withholding, can be experienced by a patient as the reenactment of a trauma and can cause unintended suffering. Moreover, neutrality does not lie in manifest comportment. Detachment that is defensively self-protective can itself express countertransference.

Frederic Levine tellingly clarifies the history of these two positions. Abstinence and benign compassion easily lose their neutrality as technical attitudes and become embroiled in analysts' superego conflicts. The former is then seen as rigidly judgmental and the latter as its wished-for opposite. Certainly the patient above experienced the analyst's unforthcoming intervention as sadistically punitive and defensively turned the tables. But the analyst was undoubtedly himself enmeshed in the kind of conflict Levine described, being responsive to a request for a schedule change, making an error about it, unnecessarily confirming a different time, treating the patient's opening remarks as referring only to the reality of the scheduling, then withholding, in the face of the patient's distress and confusion, under the guise of requesting that the patient follow the basic rule.

Olinick might here attempt to distinguish the analyst's countertransference from the possibility that he is reacting to "structural actualities" of the patient's transference. This position is not too far removed from Feldman's invocation of the patient's projective identification as "subtle unconscious provocations" which have a real effect on the analyst's state, thought, or actions. Both Feldman and Olinick would consider whether something inherent in the patient's transference was moving the analyst to enact. Olinick would wonder if the transference was thereby being actualized. He encourages us to look at larger configurations of analytic interaction. A wider focal lens, for example, might conceivably shed light upon the patient's confusion. Both the interactions and the confusion might be connected to a childhood trauma in which the patient was confused, not helped.

The lesson Bergmann distills from Ernst Kris's last papers addresses an important technical aspect of the help the patient complained of not receiving: when a patient is stuck, he reminds us, we must go beyond the id meaning of a request for help to support the integrative functions of the ego. Such an approach focuses on the actual functioning of the patient's mind. Indeed, the intervention that appeared to be helpful despite our patient's high dudgeon was one in which the analyst aided integration by reminding the patient of a sequence of associations. Although the patient may well also have been complying, the apparent effectiveness of the intervention tends to bear out Bergmann's clinical point. Was the negative transference outburst then vital to the outcome of the hour, as Kris' formulation might have it? I doubt it. The more integrative intervention alone would have enabled the patient to keep working. She might have felt, in Feldman's formulation, that the analyst was trying to understand a painful aspect of her experience in the analytic relationship that was heretofore enacted. In addition, the patient was already voicing displeasure with the analyst about his withholding—an experience that required exploration—and the rage let loose was easier of access and less conflict-laden than her longing for a nonsadistic transference object. The sadomasochistic repetition prevented these deeper issues from being attended to.

Ultimately, the patient's missing conscious feelings about the analyst's vacation and the meaning of her opening requests for something from the analyst all need to be integrated with an understanding of the deeper material. Accepting the pair's assumption, a general formulation might include: in the context of the analyst's upcoming vacation, the patient yearned for a gift from him. That wish for a gift was a revival of an oedipal wish for a baby. The analyst's vacation (and later apparent repudiation of the patient's request for help) intensified the patient's yearning, her vulnerability to hurt and humiliation as the child scorned, and her vengeful rage at both parents and the babies they created. It was probably that rage that interfered with the patient's integrative capacity. Certainly, in the hour, turned vengefully on the sadistically withholding analyst, that rage interfered with her ability to further the analytic work. However, if the pair negotiates the withholding/compliant interaction, other meanings may well be uncovered.

Every analyst has categories deemed "actual" against which to take the measure of his or her own and the patient's illusions. My understanding of the foregoing material is predicated, for example, upon theoretical assumptions about the *actual* import of unconscious conflicts and corollaries concerning their manifestation as hierarchically layered unconscious fantasies. The evidence

I use to gauge my own patients' illusion begins in the affective crucible of the analytic situation with an attempt empathically to enter the patient's experience sufficiently to understand it. That understanding involves additional actualities: the actions of the patient—for example, his or her way of speaking—and the ways that I can discern that the patient pressures me to act and feel, all in conjunction with the derivatives that emerge through the patient's free associations.

Not every psychoanalytic viewpoint specifies criteria for evidence that follow logically from the ideas upon which the espoused position is based and which identify illusory phenomena, established their meaning, and distinguish them from actualities. Nor do specifications, where they exist, necessarily either exhaust important *de facto* criteria or absolve us from facing the fact that the task of distinguishing actuality from illusion inevitably requires objective assumptions. The empathic immersion which samples the patient's subjective experience as a preliminary step to understanding requires identification, but it also requires that we move from identification to identify what in the patient's subjectivity differs from our own. Otherwise we cannot talk to the patient about his experience or the reasons it occurs. Similarly analysts who try to limit themselves to exploring the patient's psychic reality must still make an objective decision about what does *not* constitute psychic reality in order to explore it. Feldman, for instance, makes the objective decision that the experience-close analytic relationship requires the analyst to make fewer assumptions about reality. That initial decision only restricts the field where other distinctions about reality are made.

Psychoanalysts would be unwise to attempt to legislate a theoretical solution to a universal problem that has baffled philosophers. Rather, we need to identify our personal solutions to this problem and study the relative effect of those solutions on clinical work.

Gail S. Reed, Ph.D.
Issue Editor

1199 Park Avenue
New York, NY 10128

For Product Safety Concerns and Information please contact our EU representative GPSR@taylorandfrancis.com
Taylor & Francis Verlag GmbH, Kaufingerstraße 24, 80331 München, Germany

www.ingramcontent.com/pod-product-compliance
Ingram Content Group UK Ltd.
Pitfield, Milton Keynes, MK11 3LW, UK
UKHW022201190926
475702UK00003B/137
* 9 7 8 0 8 8 1 6 3 9 4 1 4 *